WAR PAINT

Fighter Nose Art
from WWII & Korea

John M. Campbell and Donna Campbell

Airlife
England

This edition first published in 1990 by Airlife Publishing, Ltd., Shrewsbury, England

ISBN 1 85310 172 9

Published by Motorbooks International, P.O. Box 2, 729 Prospect Avenue, Osceola, WI 54020, USA, 1990

Printed and bound in Singapore through PH Productions

Airlife Publishing Ltd.
101 Longden Road, Shrewsbury, England

In Memory of David Moses

To those of talent, those for whom flying seems to have been invented—whose inner mystique is so self-hypnotic that it can numb their judgment and beguile their good sense and experience when they make "one more run" because they are fascinated with flying, their self-confidence built on making intelligent decisions. All of that desire to fly simmering and compulsive is simply irresistible in their wish to "get the job done," building up their hours on their way to future dreams.

It is not merely spirit or obligation that motivates: love of flying is its own propelling force and reason.

Contents

Retired World War II Fighter Ace and author of *Happy Jack's Go Buggy.* Jack is the holder of the Silver Star, Distinguished Flying Cross with five OLCs, and the Air Medal with twelve OLCs. He is the historian of the 20th Fighter Group Association, the editor of the newsletter, *King's Cliffe Remembered,* a Director of the 8th Air Force Historical Society and the P–38 National Association.

Foreword

For thirty years John Campbell has been collecting military aircraft photos and now has a historic archive of World War II Fighter aircraft nose art, presented to you in this book.

It was quite the fad for bomber crews and fighter pilots to paint colorful markings on their aircraft, mostly humorous (especially on the bombers) some with lurid, spicy, double-meaning names combined with paintings of female forms in varying poses and apparel. Cartoon characters were also popular. It all helped boost morale.

Fighter aircraft nose art was more closely associated with the pilots who flew them. Names of wives, sweethearts, mothers, children (Capt. Glen Webb, of the 79th Fighter Squadron, 20th Fighter Group, had two young sons named Gary and Guy; his P–51 was named *GLENGARYGUY*), nicknames, lucky names and names coming from certain characteristics and other attributes of the pilots. Many names came from home towns and home states (one of my P–38s was named *Texas Terror*).

A quote from Senator Barry Goldwater's foreword in the *American Fighter Aces* album asks: "What does it take to become a fighter ace?, or for that matter just what does it require to be a fighter pilot?

"I would say first, that intense love and desire to fly an airplane all by one's self and to have complete mastery over its maneuverability, speed, both in climb and in dive and a perfect understanding of where to aim the weapon to hit the enemy. I have found invariably that those men who shot down five or more enemy aircraft were primarily very superb pilots and once having mastered that skill the rest was somewhat easy.

"The pilot who is going to become a fighter ace, if the opportunity presents itself, is a hunter—not the hunted!"

Of the thousands of pilots who had taken to the skies in World War II, only 1,284 became fighter aces. This total is composed of 761 Army Air Force and AVG aces, 383 Navy aces, 124 Marine Corps aces and sixteen Americans who became flying aces with the Royal Air Force.

Many of them and their aircraft are in this book.

John and Donna Campbell (baby boomers) have done a magnificent job of collecting these fighter aircraft nose art pictures, complete with identification of the planes, their units and histories. This book should be on every World War II enthusiast's coffee table.

We fighter pilots can talk and tell about our experiences until we are blue in the face, but nobody understands why we did what we did, except another fighter pilot.

We were proud to fly in defense of our country. It was a stirring time, as the entire American public was united and we won a great victory. Will we ever again see the *esprit de corps* that we had in those days?

After all of us World War II fighter jocks have gone on to Valhalla, the Campbells' book will be here, in perpetuity, for future generations to see the way we were.

Jack Ilfrey
A P–38 pilot who became an ace, on 26 December 1942 fighting with the 94th "Hat In The Ring" Fighter Squadron, 1st Fighter Group, 12th US Army Air Force, North Africa

Preface

This book is a tribute, a saga of an elite corps of fighter pilots whose exploits defined devotion to duty. The art painted on the aircraft here reveals the sense of pride, character and heroism of men who had to face extreme danger when fighting a dangerous enemy.

Hopefully, this effort will perpetuate our aviation heritage and the memory of those who flew, fought, laughed, cried and died from China, Burma and India to Berlin, from Paris to Rabaul. Their fighters sported as many different individual pieces of art as crews could dream up, reflecting the yearnings and thoughts men took to war.

Once again nose art is beginning to surface on modern US Air Force aircraft, yet never again are we likely to see the racy ladies, the classy chassies on active military aircraft. Today we have a more somber, perhaps less honest, approach to this form of expression of our feelings. In these pages you'll find some nostalgia for those who remember World War II as the last war with a cause which involved the entire country.

Maturity came quickly to the men who ate the dust of North Africa, felt the wind chilled German sky, suffered the bite of mosquitoes in the Pacific. They turned into hardened warriors who returned to peacetime living in an aura of fame and glory beyond their years.

It is our hope to rekindle warm memories of friendships, good feelings, of the pride and patriotism that are distinctively American, and come away with the desire to keep America strong.

Acknowledgments

At the onset of this project we did not realize the magnitude of the research involved or how far reaching it would be. We found we were not only gathering photographs of fighter aircraft, but we were also meeting a very special group of people. People who have given themselves through duty, sacrifice and devotion, to keep alive the memories and friendships that were so tightly interwoven in a time and place so far away. We wish to thank these people, not only for their assistance, without which this book could not have been written, but also for welcoming us so warmly into their homes and Associations, and sharing so freely their photos and memories. The book is about you and your devotion and service to this great country, and only exists because you have kept safe the photographs and memories of those times.

Our special appreciation and affection must go to our good friend, Jack Ilfrey, for his enthusiasm and support of this and other projects which help in the perpetuation of our national history.

Our thanks to Dr. James H. Kitchens, Archivist, History Department, and the staff of Maxwell Air Force Base Museum: Bruce A. Ashcroft, Historian Intern; Sarah F. Rawlins, Archives Technician; James S. Howard, Technical Information Specialist; and M/Sgt. Gary McDaniel USAF Reserve, for their help and patience during the week we were there.

Also our appreciation to Charles G. Worman, head of the Research Division, Air Force Museum, Wright Patterson Air Force Base, and his staff: Wesley Henry, researcher; Vivian White, researcher; Bobbie Bollinger, materials conservation; Debbie Bachman, secretary, and Joseph Ventolo, historian, for their assistance during our visit.

Our thanks to James Crowder, historian, Tinker Air Force Base, for his continuing assistance during the many years of our friendship, and his staff: Thomas M. Brewer, Jack A. Reise, and Lura M. Casey.

Also the Oklahoma Air and Space Museum Director, Don Finch, and his executive assistant, Stewart Howard, for the use of their library.

Groups and Associations we wish to thank are as follows: Joseph A. Kuhn and the P–38 National Association, Maj. S. D. Huff and the 49th Fighter Squadron, Jack T. Curtis and the 367th Fighter Group; Frank and Freida Sanders and the 79th Fighter Group, William Fowkes and the 18th Fighter Group, Rick McGowen and the 318th Fighter Group, Ed Haskamp and the 367th Fighter Group, Merle C. Olmstead and the 357th Fighter Group, Ed Bollen and the 23rd Fighter Group, and Marvin Rosvold and the 368th Fighter Group.

Individuals to whom we owe much gratitude are: James V. Crow, who opened up his immense photographic library to us; Jack Moses, artist, mentor and good friend; Wayne "Donnie" Watts for his help in and out of the lab and library; Jeffrey L. Ethell for his assistance in obtaining and identifying photographs; Paul Fornet; Robert S. Johnson; Col. Hub Zemke; Victor Veroda; Edward Janesick; J.W. Reynolds; Bill Overstreet; R. E. Casteel; E. E. Burger; Stewart Ostler of Epperson Photo and Video for his expert advice; Col. James A. Goodson and family; Ralph P. Willet; J. A. Roberts; Jack Harris; Ruth E. Havens; Garland Leonard; Arnold Fort; Mrs. W. F. Swafford; Glen J. Twist; Carl Woodard; Bill and Laura Wietelman; Lucian B. Jackson; Mike Connors of The Hobby Shop for his advice and moral support; Laxton and Freida Malcom; Nancy Heinbach; Sgt. Mark Bacon; Jane Herrera; Brenda Hackett; Levonne Higdon; Connie Robinson; Tom Ivey; Ernie McDowell; Bill Hess; and Jewel Watts.

I would at this time like to especially thank my mother Ruth and my father F. D. Campbell who have supported me through this project and my entire course of study into military aviation.

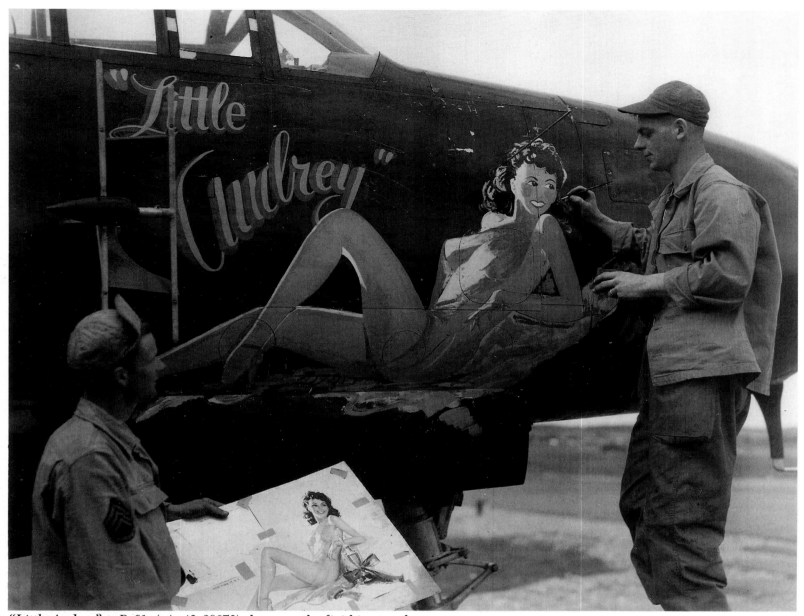

"Little Audrey", a P-61, (s/n 42–38672) shown as the finishing touches are being added to the artwork. This plane belongs to the 422nd Night Fighter Squadron, 9th Air Force. *Clark, via Crow*

Introduction

The sultry, wonderful world of warpaint is as varied as the individuals who dressed up and decorated the aircraft and the feelings of the men who flew them into combat. Though this variety is staggering, common themes run through them all from World War II to the end of the Korean War when the genre all but left the scene.

Humor, pathos, slogans, girls, cartoons, nicknames, hometowns, girls, patriotism, dishing it to the enemy, warriors, girls, youthful bravado, girls . . . these transcended nationality as both Allies and Axis pilots went to war in their individually marked chariots. Men at war separated from home, family, loved ones and a familiar way of life sought ways to personalize and escape the very harsh business surrounding them. For the most part they thought about women, represented on the sides of aircraft

Pinups like this were in many cases the inspiration for the artwork found on the aircraft. *Jack Ilfrey*

This pinup titled "Sport Model," like "Caught in the Draft" was the work of Elvgren. Although the pinups pictured here were considered risque at the time, once transferred to the nose of a plane gave the word risque a new meaning. *Jack Ilfrey*

This type of pinup art was found in mess halls, rec rooms, and living quarters. Sometimes it was the only thing for miles that was pleasant to the eyes. It was a reminder of home and the ladies that so anxiously awaited their return. *John McGuire*

This is the rec room of the 49th Fighter Squadron, 14th Fighter Group. Starting on the left in the mid section of the photo is a record board showing the unofficial emblem of the 49th, the "Fork-tailed Devils", over the book case are characters of "Beetle Bailey", followed by a large mural of one of the more popular pinup poses.

in the most tender of ways to the most degrading. These men spent many hours longing for the tenderness a woman could bring to their lives . . . and for the sexual pleasure they could provide. Whether top level commanders ordered it off the aircraft or not, the men let their feelings flow onto their machines.

The warpaint represented in each of the aircraft here provides a picture into the soul of its crew through captions recalling the fighter jock and his crew. Pilots' strong points, specialties and their running scoreboard of triumphs in combat were painted in youthful blood and guts fashion with almost innocent bravado . . . but we'll also read of those who paid the supreme sacrifice for freedom.

During World War II a variety of victory markings appeared to let crew and unit know just how well a pilot did in combat. A German or Japanese flag denoted a single aircraft shot down but the painted symbols, usually on the left side of the aircraft, came in the form of Luftwaffe eagles, swastikas, Maltese crosses, red meatballs, rising suns. A bomb represented a single tactical bombing mission, umbrellas stood for top cover of aircraft or troops on the ground while top hats were for protective fighter escort of bombers.

During the first years of the war, low level fighter missions were considered risky enough to be dicing with death, which became "dicing" for short. Soon a pair of dice appeared to mark such missions and by the time low level photo recon missions became standard, the term was transferred. There were also camera outlines for each photo recce mission flown. The stencil of a locomotive would signify a pilot had destroyed a steam engine, the same would be true for a tank silhouette. When brooms started appearing on fighter noses they denoted fighter sweeps while ships signified those sunk. Fighter sweeps usually resulted in some form of combat since it was a free-ranging search-and-destroy mission against anything that moved on or over enemy territory. These sweeps were, at the same time, exhilarating and terrifying for the pilot and the enemy.

As their aircraft reflected, fighter pilots of both wars were busy strafing, bombing, hunting for aerial kills and protecting friendly aircraft, airfields, supply lines and troops. But the grounds crews were just as busy trying to make sure the aircraft they had generously loaned to the pilot was on the line each day and ready to bring him home—there is never enough credit to be given to these men who worked ten hours for every hour the pilot flew. The fame and glory attached to the fighter pilot overshadowed his faithful ground pounders, but this usually did not prevent enlisted men and officers from becoming devoted friends. Each needed the other to make the mission successful, and a pilot's crew would experience as much pride for a victory, knowing they were behind the guns as well. As a result, nose art was often the choice of the ground crew rather than the pilot. Some units made room for both by having the pilot's art on the left side and the ground crew's on the right. Unique among fighters, the P-38 Lightning had three noses to adorn, allowing a separate canvas for the pilot, crew chief, armorer and radio man.

The demands placed on crews from the various fighter commands were always the same: keep the fighters in the air, pound bridges and supply lines, attack fighter

This club is also decorated with popular pinups of the day.

bases in the heart of enemy territory, hit and hit again. Keep the enemy harassed to the point he can't think of anything but unconditional surrender. With the buzzing hornets over his head the enemy couldn't eat, couldn't fight and couldn't even move.

Through the warpaint of these men, we'll get an intimate look at the lives they led and the dreams they held dear for themselves and those they left at home. May we heed the terrible lessons of war and peace they paid for.

The living quarters of these men were luxurious in comparison to a fox hole.

JOKER, a P-40 piloted by 1st Lt. Robert M. Bellman of the 75th
Fighter Squadron, 23rd Fighter Group. On September 25, 1944,
Bellman damaged two Japanese Zero fighters (Mitsubishi A6M3).
He was later killed in a P-51 landing accident. *Ed Bollen*

China-Burma-India Theater

The American Volunteer Group (AVG) in China was essentially the reality of one man's faith in the effectiveness of pursuit (fighter) aircraft. Clarie Lee Chennault, a brilliant student and teacher in the US Army Air Corps Tactical School during the 1930s, was expected to adhere to the party line: "bombardment, once in the air, cannot be stopped." Instead, he devised and implemented procedures for detecting and reporting incoming bombers, then intercepting and destroying or repulsing them by pursuits, publishing his theories in 1935 under the title "The Role of Defensive Pursuit."

So at odds were his theories with the doctrine of the Air Corps leaders above him, that Chennault retired from the service in 1937 after an offer from the Chinese government to rebuild the Chinese Air Force. With the Japanese invasion of China that year, Chiang Kai-shek authorized Chennault to buy modern American fighters and, by 1940, to begin hiring trained Americans as a nucleus for effective defense. In the end, the only fighters available were export Curtiss P-40Bs released by the British in exchange for the promise of newer models at a later date.

Although Chennault was not a great fan of the P-40, John Alison's demonstration flight so impressed the members of the Chinese purchasing mission they immediately told Chennault they needed 100 of the planes. His reply was typical, "No, what you need is a hundred Johnny Alisons."

In his efforts to recruit Americans from the US armed services to fly the new P-40s, Chennault met the strong opposition he had been so accustomed to in his Air Corps days. However, with the blessing of President Franklin D. Roosevelt, the AVG was born, becoming immortal as the "Flying Tigers."

Though they trained hard during 1941, the AVG did not enter combat until thirteen days after the Japanese attack on Pearl Harbor. That first mission was crammed with its share of confusion, but the Japanese bombers, facing opposition for the first time, were turned back without hitting the target.

The AVG was composed of three different units. The 1st Pursuit Squadron, nicknamed "Adam & Eve" for the first pursuit in history, scored a total of 98.5 confirmed, twenty-one unconfirmed and five damaged. Among its aces were Robert H. Neale (15.5 kills), Robert L. Little (10.5) and Gregory "Pappy" Boyington (six with AVG, twenty-two with USMC). The 2nd Pursuit Squadron, the "Panda Bears," accounted for 64.5 kills, eight unconfirmed and one damaged, with aces such as David "Tex" Hill

(12.25 with AVG, seven with AAF) and Edward F. Rector (6.5 with AVG, three with AAF). The 3rd Pursuit Squadron, the "Hells Angels," ended up with sixty-eight confirmed, fourteen unconfirmed and twenty-seven damaged and aces like Charles H. Older (ten with AVG, 8.5 with AAF) and R. T. Smith (nine).

Considering that only fourteen AVG aircraft were lost in action, the group's success in combat ranks it as one of the most effective fighter units ever fielded. This is even more amazing since the P-40 was supposedly inferior overall to the Japanese Zero. Chennault's genius as a fighter tactician was proven in spades—and was proven time and again until the end of the war.

On July 4, 1942, the AVG contracts expired, and the Flying Tigers ceased to exist. That day the USAAF 23rd Fighter Group was activated at Kunming and a few members of the AVG stayed on to give newly arrived AAF personnel the benefit of their combat experience. Chennault rejoined the AAF as a brigadier general to command the China Air Task Force, which later became the 14th Air Force in March 1943.

The CBI Theater was by far the most difficult to keep supplied. With both the 10th and 14th Air Forces active deep inside humid, thick mountain ranges, the only realistic method was aerial transport across the Hump, the Himalaya mountain ranges that separated the Middle East from China. In spite of the continual lack of proper food, housing and other basic necessities, fuel and ordnance became the overwhelming need. Transport pilots did battle with some of the world's worst weather, becoming the shaft of an aerial spear tipped by the CBI fighter pilot.

Primarily an air-to-ground theater, the CBI did not produce the string of high scoring aces found elsewhere. Though this frustrated crews, the effective support of ground troops was crucial to keeping the Japanese at bay. The Curtiss P-40 remained the area's primary fighter until midwar, when P-51s, P-38s, P-47s and P-61s began arriving to re-equip several groups. Many pilots considered the P-40 to be a better fighter than the P-51 for the theater. Though slower, the P-40 was more maneuverable and did not have as much vulnerable liquid cooling plumbing. This was crucial during ground support work and Mustangs went down more often than Warhawks when hit by small arms fire.

The 10th Air Force lists but nine aces, reflecting its long, hard years of continual fighter-bomber work. Five of the nine and the two highest scorers, Walter F. Duke (eight kills) and Hampton E. Boggs (nine kills), flew Lightnings with the 459th Fighter Squadron. This sole

P–38 unit in the 10th AF was known as the "Twin Dragons" due to the garish green-headed monsters they would paint down the side of each engine boom. The 311th Fighter Bomber Group arrived in the theater with A-36As, the dive bombing version of the Allison-powered Mustang, then converted over to P-51As. The group produced two aces with James J. England (ten kills) being the highest scorer. On the deck the Allison Mustangs proved to be among the best fighters of the war.

By contrast the 14th Air Force produced over fifty aces, reflecting the higher number of fighter units and the vast area it had to cover. By far the majority served with the 23rd Fighter Group, the Flying Tigers' successor, which continued to paint the famous shark mouth on its P-40s. This fierce apparition quickly spread to other units and other aircraft, particularly the P-51, and though other theaters of war used it, the shark mouth remained the hallmark of Chennault's command. The names of the 14th's top aces are still recognizable today—John "Pappy" Herbst (fifteen air, two ground kills), Edward O.

McComas (fourteen air, three ground), Robert L. Scott (thirteen air, one ground kill and author of *God Is My Co-pilot*), Bruce K. Holloway (thirteen), John R. Alison (ten). Several aces with the Flying Tigers managed to more than double their scores in the 14th.

While nose art was scarce during the early years of the war, the basic trend continued until the end—an aggressive, demeaning challenge to the Japanese with figures tearing the Japanese flag, cartoon characters using the rising sun as a latrine or Tojo with buck teeth and thick glasses getting the boot. The rudder art in the CBI usually centered around nude women while the shark mouths came in quite a variety from upturned or downturned mouths, sharp teeth or long sabre teeth, some seeming to smile, others grimacing. Names for anything from girfriends and wives to inanimate objects were painted on according to the dictates of pilot and ground crews who found the canvas of their personal aircraft a welcome relief from one of the toughest theaters of war.

Mrs. Virginia, a P–51 of the 1st Air Commando Group. The top aircraft in the photo, a P-51, s/n 43–6189, is the plane of Col. Phillip G. Cochran, Commanding Officer (CO) of the group. *AFM*

Cheese Cake Chassis, a P-51 piloted by Lt. B. Mayer of the 2nd Air Commando Group, 10th Air Force in Cox's Bazaar, Burma, 1945. *Mayer, via Crow*

Miss Margie Sue, "*Rebel Gal*", a P-51, s/n 44–15417, of the 2nd Air Commando Group, 10th Air Force, Cox's Bazaar, Burma, 1945. *AFM*

Pictured here are Flying Tigers Lt. John R. Alison credited with six aerial victories, Col. David L. "Tex" Hill with six aerial victories, Capt. Albert J. Baumler with five aerial victories, and Capt. Mack A. Mitchell with four aerial victories. *Tex Hill*

Tommy's Dad, a P-40, piloted by Lt. Col. John C. "Pappy" Herbst of the 74th Fighter Squadron, 23rd Fighter Group 14th Air Force. Herbst named his plane after his son Tommy. Herbst is credited with eighteen aerial victories. *Charlie Cook, via Crow*

This P-40, *KING BOOGIE*, is pictured with distinguished members of the 75th Fighter Squadron. Sitting on the airplane are: Maj. Goss (6 kills), Lt. Col. Alison (6 kills), and Capt. Pryor (5 kills). In the front row are: Maj. Griffin (7 kills), Capt. Mitchell (4 kills), Capt. Hampshire, Jr. (13 kills) and Capt. Blackstone (3 kills). *Col. Griffin, via OASM*

A P-40E, s/n 41-36402, of the 16th Fighter Squadron, 23rd Fighter Group. *AFM*

This P-40, *HELLZAPOPPIN*, was piloted by 1st Lt. Joseph H. Griffin of the 75th Fighter Squadron, 23rd Fighter Group. Griffin is credited with seven kills—three in the CBI and four in the ETO where he flew a P-38. *Ed Bollen*

Pictured is the 75th's flight line at Kunming. The 75th was later to paint their spinners white. Note the 75th insignia on the tail. According to Ed Bollen, the 75th had the best looking shark mouths of any of the squadrons. *Ed Bollen*

This P-40 dummy aircraft was one of several which the 75th Fighter Squadron had at Chinkiang. They were made of woven bamboo and looked quite real from the air. Donbien, the Chinese boy closest to the prop was the squadron mascot. *Ed Bollen*

The Duchess, a P-40 piloted by 1st Lt. Leonard E. Aylesworth of the 75th Fighter Squadron, 23rd Fighter Group. On May 27, 1944, Aylesworth shot down a Tojo (Nakajima Ki-44). *Ed Bollen*

This P-51, *HILLZAPOPPIN*, was piloted by Meredith Hill of the 75th Fighter Squadron, 23rd Fighter Group. His crew chief was Ed Justin. This picture was taken after the war at Hangchow. *Ed Bollen*

P-51, *MALICIOUS MAUREEN*, was piloted by Herman "Kirk" Kirkpatrick of the 75th Fighter Squadron, 23rd Fighter Group. His crew chief was Oscar Carpenter. *Ed Bollen*

ROSALIE, a P-51 piloted by Lt. Joshua D. "Chief" Sanford of the 75th Fighter Squadron, 23rd Fighter Group. Joshua and Crew Chief, Myron Funmaker, were both Native Americans. Sanford is credited with destroying one Oscar (Nakajima Ki-43). *Ed Bollen*

This P-51, *Patricia*, was piloted by Joe Summey. His crew chief was Harold Freeman. Both were in the 75th Fighter Squadron, 23rd Fighter Group. *Ed Bollen*

Eadie Mae, a P-51 piloted by 1st Lt. Edward J. Bollen of the 75th Fighter Squadron, 23rd Fighter Group. Pictured with Bollen is his crew chief, S/Sgt. William L. Heath, at Tsingchen, China, May 1945. *Ed Bollen*

LOPE'S HOPE 3RD, a P-51 piloted by 1st Lt. Donald S. Lopez of the 75th Fighter Squadron, 23rd Fighter Group. Pictured left to right are: Wiltz Segura, Don Lopez, Bryan Glass. Lt. Lopez is credited with five aerial victories. *Ed Bollen*

ANNA LEE, LOUISIANA LADY, a P-51 piloted by Capt. Sam Dance of the 75th Fighter Squadron, 23rd Fighter Group. Dance was killed in a mission over Hangyang. *Ed Bollen*

DAKOTA MAID, a P-51 piloted by 1st Lt. Russ Fleming of the 75th Fighter Squadron, 23rd Fighter Group. On January 14, 1945, Lt. Fleming damaged a Tojo over Hankow, China. *Ed Bollen*

This P-51, *DUDE*, was piloted by 1st Lt. Donald "Skip" Stanfield of the 75th Fighter Squadron, 23rd Fighter Group. Stanfield is credited with destroying one Oscar and damaging another. He later served in Korea and Vietnam. *Ed Bollen*

Miss Kitty/Rosie The RED DEVIL, a P-51 piloted by Lt. John "Rosie" Rosenbaum. Lt. Rosenbaum damaged a Zero on September 16, 1944, while flying a P-40 and an Oscar on November 11, 1944, while flying a P-51. Rosenbaum served in Korea and later Vietnam. *Ed Bollen*

The Flying Mouse, a P-51 piloted by 2nd Lt. James "Mouse" Carter of the 75th Fighter Squadron, 23rd Fighter Group. His crew chief was Ed Jones. On November 10, 1944, James destroyed an Oscar over Nanyo, China. *Ed Bollen*

LITTLE NELL, a P-51 piloted by 1st Lt. Bill Walterman of the 75th Fighter Squadron, 23rd Fighter Group. Walterman is credited with damage to an Oscar over Hankow January 14, 1945. After the war he was killed while flying a P-51 for the Texas ANG. *Ed Bollen*

THE STREAK, a P-51 piloted by 1st Lt. Jesse B. Gray of the 75th Fighter Squadron, 23rd Fighter Group. Gray is credited with one destroyed, four probable, and five damaged. *Ed Bollen*

The P-51, *ALTA MARIE*, "that's my baby" was piloted by 2nd Lt. Gordon E. Willis, 75th Fighter Squadron, 23rd Fighter Group. Willis destroyed two Zeroes and damaged one Oscar. *Ed Bollen*

BUTCH, a P-51 piloted by 1st Lt. Robert E. Smith of the 75th Fighter Squadron, 23rd Fighter Group. Lt. Smith is credited with a probable Oscar on September 21, 1944, over Sinshih, China. *Ed Bollen*

Little Rock III, a P-51 piloted by Charles Glanville. *Ed Bollen*

The 75th Fighter Squadron flight line at Chinkiang with a long line of P-51s, beginning with *Japeth IV* followed by *Little Jeep*, with the tail code 187. *Ed Bollen*

This P-40, *Little Jeep*, was piloted by Capt. Forrest "Pappy" Parham of the 75th Fighter Squadron, 23rd Fighter Group. Parham is credited with five aerial victories. *Ed Bollen*

THE TALKING DOG, a P-51 piloted by Frederick Graber. *Ed Bollen*

"*JINX*", a P-40K-S of the 25th Fighter Squadron, 51st Fighter Group. The 51st fought from the Assam Valley, India, in 1944.

P-40, piloted by Maj. Edward M. Nollemeyer of the 26th Fighter Squadron, 51st Fighter Group. Nollemeyer was one of the few members of the 26th to achieve the title of ace. His total claims were five destroyed, four probable, and damage to an Oscar. *AFM*

A P-47D-23-RA, s/n 42-27447, piloted by Lt. Col. S. Smith, Jr., showing the insignia of the 80th Fighter Group on the side of his plane. *MAFB*

Haleakala, a P-38 piloted by Lt. H. H. "Lighthouse Harry" Sealy of the 459th Fighter Squadron, 80th Fighter Group. Notice the dragon markings on the twin booms. Sealy was from Hawaii and thus the name "Haleakala", meaning house of the sun. *Victor Veroda*

"*Haleakala II*," pictured with the pilot, Lt. H. H. Sealy, and members of the ground crew. This P-38 is likely s/n 42-67291, since Sealy's last scores were made in that plane. These scores include one probable, one destroyed, and one damaged—all Oscars. *Victor Veroda*

"*BABY BONNIE*," a P-38 piloted by Capt. Victor Veroda of the 459th Fighter Squadron (also known as the "Twin Dragons"), 80th Fighter Group. This photo was taken in Chittagong, India. *Victor Veroda*

Geronimo II, a P-38 belonging to the 459th Fighter Squadron, 80th Fighter Group. The tail code is number 81. *Meyer, via Crow*

This side of *Geronimo II* shows the artwork and a partial serial number of 2356. *Meyer, via Crow*

This P–38, *DIXIE BELL III*, was piloted by 2nd Lt. James G. Harris of the 459th Fighter Squadron, 80th Fighter Group. Harris destroyed two Oscars and a Lili (Kawasaki Ki–48) twin engined-light bomber. He also damaged three Oscars. *Victor Veroda*

PATSY, MARGIE, MARY, a P–38 belonging to the 459th Fighter Squadron, 80th Fighter Group. *Victor Veroda*

This P–38, *Miss-V*, was piloted by Capt. Walter F. Duke of the 459th Fighter Squadron, 80th Fighter Group. Duke is credited with ten confirmed and two probable aerial victories and five aircraft damaged. *Victor Veroda*

MELBA LOU was the P–38 piloted by Capt. Hampton E. Boggs of the 459th Fighter Squadron, 80th Fighter Group. Boggs is credited with nine aerial victories, including four Zeroes, four Oscars and a Jill (Nakajima B6N) attack bomber. *Victor Veroda*

Sluggo-V, a P–38 flown by Maj. Maxwell H. Glenn of the 459th Fighter Squadron, 80th Fighter Group. Maj. Glenn is credited with 7.5 aerial victories. *Victor Veroda*

DONNA MARIE, a P–38 belonging to the 459th Fighter Squadron, 80th Fighter Group. The damage shown here is the results of a landing accident. Note the way the metal tore at the seam. *Victor Veroda*

A P–40N of the 80th Fighter Group appears very unusual, only the jaw and teeth are showing because the upper cowling, having been damaged, was replaced by a piece that bears an eye like those on shark-mouthed P–40s. *E. McDowell*

These P–40's of the 80th Fighter Group are lined up on the runway at Upper Assam, India. There are skulls as far as a man can see, but notice the subtle differences in each. *E. McDowell*

Miss Frances III, a P–40 of the 80th Fighter Group shown on the flight line at Nogaghuli Air Base, Upper Assam, India, May 5, 1944, with many other similarly painted P–40s.

This P–40 of the 80th Fighter Group, Upper Assam, India, was piloted by Col. Ivan W. McElroy. Notice the writing *Merry Xmas "Tojo"* on the bomb. Photo taken in December, 1944.

This P–40N, *Flung Dung,* shows its own variation of the skull which decorated the aircraft of the 89th Fighter Squadron, 80th Fighter Group, 10th Air Force. Each of the aircraft was unique in its version. *MAFB*

Jinx Falkenburg, a P–47 of the 81st Fighter Group in China. Actress Jinx Falkenburg (right) poses beside the aircraft named in her honor. *B. Hess*

Pictured here is Hampton Boggs, the third CO of the 459th Fighter Squadron, 80th Fighter Group, 10th Air Force, standing by a P-38 painted with the familiar "Pistol Packin' Mama". *Meyer, via Crow*

GOLDEN GATE *in 48?*, a P-38 belonging to the 459th Fighter Squadron, 80th Fighter Group. *AFM*

California Redhead, a P-38 piloted by J. L. Huesman of the 459th Fighter Squadron, 80th Fighter Group. Another major theme of nose art was the women that pilots and crew left behind. *Victor Veroda*

BEACH RAT, a P-38 piloted by F. Flanders of the 459th Fighter Squadron, 80th Fighter Group. *Victor Veroda*

This aerial shot of the P-38 *THE SAN JOAQUIN SIREN* provides a good view of the pilot in the cockpit and the dragon motif of the 459th Fighter Squadron. *Crow*

This P-38 bears the emblem of the 459th Fighter Squadron, the Twin Dragons. It was the aircraft of Victor Veroda, pictured here with his plane. *Victor Veroda*

"GENTLE ANNIE", a P–51 piloted by Col. Harold J. Rau, CO of the 20th Fighter Group is first in an assortment of nine aircraft all being flown by group COs. This photo was taken at Bottisham Airfield, Cambridgeshire in August of 1944. The aircraft pictured are as follows: *"GENTLE ANNIE"* (code MC-R, s/n 44–13337) Col. H. J. Rau; *STRAW BOSS 2* (code PE-X, s/n 44–14111) piloted by Col. James Mayden; *WHACK*, a P–47 (code LM-S, s/n 42–75541) piloted by Col. Dave Schilling; *DAQUAKE*, a P–51 (code CL-P, s/n 44–14291) piloted by Col. John McGinn; *JUDY*, a P–47 (code PJ-T, s/n 42–26415) piloted by Col. Phil Tukey; a P–47 (code LH-E, s/n 42–28422) piloted by Col. Ben Rimerman. Behind and at the back are a P–38 J2R flown to Bottisham by Hub Zemke and Col. Fred Gray's P–47 *MR. TED* (code HL-Z) of the 78th Fighter Group. *USAF, via Warren Bodie*

European Theater

When war broke out in Europe in September 1939 the United States was strongly isolationist. Nevertheless, an increasing number of American young men joined the Royal Air Force, most through Canada, particularly after the Battle of Britain in the summer of 1940 when a small band of RAF pilots stopped the Luftwaffe. By 1941 most of these Americans were gathered into three Eagle Squadrons (No. 71, No. 121 and No. 133), flying Hurricanes and Spitfires.

With the entry of the United States into the war, the 8th Air Force was created to initiate American combat operations from England and the European Theater of Operations (ETO) with a small nucleus of B–17 bomb groups and a few fighter groups. By August 1942 the 1st and 14th Fighter Groups, flying P–38Fs, and the 31st and 52nd Fighter Groups, flying reverse lend-lease Spitfire Vs, began to see combat, but, with the coming invasion of North Africa, each of these units was transferred to the Mediterranean by October.

The core of American fighter experience remained in the Eagle Squadrons, and 8th AF planners soon arranged to have all three transferred, along with their Spitfires, into the new American 8th Air Force in September as the 4th Fighter Group. These battle-tested men soon had their names attached to increasing scores—Don Blakeslee (11.5 air, 1.5 ground kills), Don Gentile (19.83 air, seven ground), John Godfrey (16.3 air, eighteen ground), Ralph "Kidd" Hofer (fifteen air, fourteen ground), Freddie Glover (10.3 air, 12.5 ground), Duane Beeson (19.3 air, 4.75 ground), Jim Goodson (twelve air, thirteen ground), Willard Millikan (thirteen air, two ground), Deacon Hively (twelve air, two ground), Pierce McKennon (eleven air, 9.68 ground) and a long string of others. By the time the war ended, the 4th had become the highest scoring (including ground kills) group in the Army Air Forces.

The 4th was the 8th's only operational fighter group until March 1943 when the former RAF pilots gave up their beloved Spitfires for the massive Republic P–47C Thunderbolt, which could escort the bombers deeper into enemy territory, and the 56th and 78th Fighter Groups arrived with their own P–47s. As more bomb groups arrived in England, additional Thunderbolt units were sent to keep up the escort duties.

Early on, however, it was obvious the Thunderbolt could not provide protection for deep penetration. As a result, the 8th AFs bombers suffered massive losses from August through October 1943. The 55th Fighter Group brought its P–38 Lightnings to England and started flying missions in October while the 20th Group started flying Lightnings in action during late December.

More fighter units were slated for England but none were more welcome than the 354th Fighter Group, on loan from the tactical 9th Air Force with the new Merlin-powered P–51B Mustang. At last, the 8th possessed a fighter that had outstanding range with a good mix of maneuverability and firepower to take on the Luftwaffe over its own fields. The 8th's first Mustang unit, the 357th Fighter Group, started flying in February 1944, along with an increasing number of other fighter groups, just in time for the 8th's major effort to put the Luftwaffe on the ropes.

During the periods of 20 to 25 February 1944, in what became known as "Big Week," and the first daylight missions to Berlin from 4 to 9 March, American and German fighter pilots slugged it out as never before. Though the Luftwaffe was not put out of the war, the Americans ran up a string of impressive victories through April making household names of aces like Gabby Gabreski (top 8th ace with twenty-eight aerial and 2.5 ground kills), George Preddy (26.83 air, five ground), Bob Johnson (twenty-seven), John C. Meyer (twenty-four air, thirteen ground), Dave Schilling (22.5 air, 10.5 ground) and Bud Marhurin (19.75 air).

As an incentive to get fighter pilots to risk their lives in strafing missions, credits for ground kills were authorized by 8th Air Force Fighter Command, and a free-for-all started to see who could get the most ground kills. Many became ground aces, but the king was Elwyn Righetti (twenty-seven ground, 7.5 air), followed closely by Joe Thury 25.5 ground, 2.5 air), William Cullerton (twenty-one ground, six air) and John Landers, (twenty ground, 8.5 air). Ground credits were not "sitting ducks". The German airfields were well defended by accurate flak and small arms fire, and most of the top aces that were shot down, fell while strafing. Their ranks include Gabreski, Godfrey, Goodson, and even expert strafers like Righetti and Thury!

By mid 1944 nothing that moved was safe on the continent as Allied fighters and medium bombers went after heavily defended airfields, trains, trucks, motorcycles, horse-drawn carts—it didn't matter. While the P–51 reigned supreme in the high altitude battles waged over Germany by the 8th AF, the rugged P–47, in the hands of 9th AF pilots, became the supreme ground attack fighter of the war.

All fighter groups in Europe had strong rivalries for the most aircraft or ground targets destroyed. In the 8th this rivalry rose to new heights when the 4th Fighter Group, under Don Blakeslee with P–51s, and the 56th Fighter Group, Hub Zemke's Wolfpack with P–47s, tried to outdo each other every month. By the end of the war both groups had managed to destroy more than 1,000 German aircraft on the ground and the air. The 4th came out ahead with 1,052.5 claims, but the 56th had more aerial victories and produced the most aces.

In the rich hunting grounds over Germany, American pilots found their adversaries to be increasingly inexperienced—meat on the table—resulting in climbing scores. When the war ended in May 1945, the 8th had produced 261 aces. The 9th, being primarily a ground-support air force, came up with sixty-nine aces, the

healthy majority having been with the 354th Fighter Group which had been "on loan" to the 8th in order to get its Merlin Mustangs on escort duty. The 354th's Glenn T. Eagleston emerged as the top 9th AF ace with 18.5 victories, followed by 353rd Squadron mates Don Beerbower (15.5), Jack T. Bradley (fifteen), Ken Dahlberg (fourteen) and Bruce Carr (fourteen). Former Flying Tiger ace (6.3 kills) James H. Howard flew a combat tour with the 354th, ending up with another six kills and the only Medal of Honor awarded to a fighter pilot in the ETO.

Without the American fighter pilots of the 8th and 9th Air Force to keep the Luftwaffe at bay and cripple the enemy's movements on the ground, VE Day would have been much longer in coming.

Miss DALLAS, a P–47 (code QP-K, s/n 42–7876) piloted by Capt. Victor J. France of the 334th Fighter Squadron, 4th Fighter Group, 8th Air Force. France is credited with 4.33 aerial victories. *AFM*

EAGER BEAVER, a P–47, (code VF-M, s/n 41–6529) piloted by Lt. Jack L. Raphael, 336th Fighter Squadron, 4th Fighter Group. Aircraft also bears the name *Miss BETH. Crow*

Lucky/Reggie's Reply, a P–47 piloted by Capt. John T. Godfrey of the 336th Fighter Squadron, 4th Fighter Group. Godfrey's dog, Lucky, sits on the wing of the plane named for him and Godfrey's brother, Reggie, killed in the North Atlantic sea war. Godfrey scored 16.33 aerial victories. *Crow*

Arizona Pete, a P–47D (code VF-F, s/n 41–6539) piloted by Lt. Kenneth D. Peterson, 336th Fighter Squadron, 4th Fighter Group parked on Debden ramp, 1943. *Arizona Pete* not only has nose art, but its 200 gallon belly tank also carries a message to the enemy. *AFM*

THIS ABOVE ALL, a P-47 piloted by Lt. James F. Steele, 335th Fighter Squadron, 4th Fighter Group. Lt. Steele is credited with one aerial victory, March 5, 1944, when he shot down an Fw 200 in a P-51B, WD-T, 43-6959. *AFM*

Shangrila, a P-51 piloted by Capt. Don S. Gentile, of the 336th Fighter Squadron, 4th Fighter Group. Gentile is credited with 21.84 aerial victories. Gentile survived the war, but was killed January 28, 1951, in an air accident. *M. Bacon*

Salem Representative, a P-51 piloted by Lt. Ralph Hofer of the 334th Fighter Squadron, 4th Fighter Group. In less than eight months, from his first mission on October 8, 1943 (scoring his first kill) until he was KIA on July 2, 1944, he scored 15 aerial victories. *AFM*

Sunny VIII, a P-51 (code VF-S, s/n 44-72181) piloted by Col. Everett W. Stewart, CO of the 4th Fighter Group. He flew for the 355th Fighter Squadron before becoming CO and scored 8.83 aerial victories. *AFM*

RIDGE RUNNER III, a P-51 (code WD-A, s/n 44-14221) piloted by Maj. Pierce W. McKennon of the 335th Fighter Squadron, 4th Fighter Group. Maj. McKennon is credited with eleven aerial victories. *AFM*

A P-51 (code VF-B, s/n 44-14787) piloted by Maj. Fred W. Glover, CO of the 336th Fighter Squadron, 4th Fighter Group. Maj. Glover is credited with 10.33 aerial victories, three of which were on November 21, 1944. *Olmstead*

Pistol Packin' Mamma, a P–47 shown with pilot, Capt. Fonzo "Snuffy" Smith of the 335th Fighter Squadron, 4th Fighter Group. Smith is credited with three aerial victories. *AFM*

The DEACON, a P–47 flown by Maj. Howard "Deacon" Hively of the 334th Fighter Squadron, 4th Fighter Group. Hively is credited with twelve aerial victories. *AFM*

"HELL'S BELLE", a P–47D (code WD-V, s/n 42–74726) piloted by 1st Lt. Charles F. Anderson of the 335th Fighter Squadron, 4th Fighter Group. Lt. Anderson is credited with ten aerial victories. *AFM*

A P–47D with Maj. James A. Goodson of the 336th Fighter Squadron, 4th Fighter Group. Goodson is credited with twelve aerial victories, one damaged, and one probable. *Jim Goodson*

An earlier *Shangri-La*, (code VF-T, s/n 43–6913) piloted by Capt. Gentile. He is shown with Crew Chief S/Sgt. John Ferra. Capt. Gentile was the leading ace of the 336th. *OASM*

BUCKEYE-DON, Don Gentile's Spitfire. Gentile is credited with an Fw 190 while flying this aircraft. He flew Spitfires with No. 133 Eagle Squadron and the 4th. *AFM*

Tony, a P–47 of the 5th Emergency Rescue Squadron, pictured on a patrol of the North Sea. It is equipped with a dinghy packed under the wing and smoke markers under the fuselage. *AFM*

OKIE BLOKE IV, a P–51 piloted by Capt. William W. Smith of the 79th Fighter Squadron, 20th Fighter Group, 8th Air Force. Capt. Smith is credited with two aerial victories and was awarded the Air Medal and two OLC. *MAFB*

"Posse", a P–38J–10–LO (code 42–68010) piloted by 1st Lt. Robert E. Miles of the 55th Fighter Squadron, 20th Fighter Group. He was awarded the DFC as well as Air Medal with three OLC. *MAFB*

HAPPY JACK'S GO BUGGY, a P–51D piloted by Maj. Ilfrey, now CO of the 79th Fighter Squadron, 20th Fighter Group. Ilfrey also piloted a P–38 named *Happy Jack's Go Buggy*. *AFM*

Wilda, a P–38 piloted by Maj. Merle B. Nichols of the 79th Fighter Squadron, 20th Fighter Group. Maj. Nichols is credited with three aerial victories. He is pictured here shortly after a near-fatal mission over Germany. *MAFB*

MURPH III, the P–38 piloted by Capt. Maurice R. McLary of the 55th Fighter Squadron, 20th Fighter Group. Capt. McLary is pictured here with Sgt. Charles R. Jordon. He is credited with three aerial victories and holds the DFC, Air Medal and three OLC. *MAFB*

Lucky Lady, the P-38 piloted by 1st Lt. Arthur W. Heiden. Looking down from the side of the ship is a pinup of Laraine Day. Lt. Heiden was credited with 0.5 aerial victories while in the 79th Fighter Squadron, 20th Fighter Group. *MAFB*

LIL' HENRY, a P-38 piloted by Maj. Maurice R. McLary. While serving with the 55th Fighter Squadron, McLary destroyed three enemy aircraft and damaged three more. On August 4, 1944, McLary took command of the 77th Fighter Squadron. *MAFB*

BOBBY, a P-38J piloted by Lt. Robert H. Reimensnider of the 20th Fighter Group. Shown with the pilot are Sgt. Carl T. Penkalski (left), assistant crew chief, and S/Sgt. Herbert C. Macrow, crew chief. *MAFB*

Mama's Boy, a P-38 of the 20th Fighter Group, 55th Fighter Squadron. *AFM*

Jeanne, a P-38 (code KI-N, s/n 43-28430) piloted by Capt. Roy Scrutchfield of the 55th Fighter Squadron, 20th Fighter Group. *AFM*

A later *JEANNE*, P-38 piloted by Capt. Roy Scrutchfield, 55th Fighter Squadron, 20th Fighter Group. *AFM*

Little Lady, a P-51D (code K1-K), piloted by 2nd Lt. James S. Reynolds of the 55th Fighter Squadron, 20th Fighter Group. Lt. Reynolds is credited with 0.5 aerial victories. *AFM*

Chattanooga Choo-Choo, a P-51D piloted by Lt. Pogue of the 77th Fighter Squadron, 20th Fighter Group. *AFM*

Snuggle Bunny, a P-51D, with members of the 20th Fighter Group. Rear: Green, Russell, Jones, Walker, Brocies, Lirosanti, and Signor. Front: Turner, Peters, Taylor, Quinlan, Kelli, Ballen, Mead, Duffy. Note the small painting of "Sleepy Time Gal" on the fuselage. *AFM*

BLACK'S BIRD, a P-51D piloted by 1st Lt. Richard H. Black of the 79th Fighter Squadron, 20th Fighter Group. Lt. Black is credited with one aerial victory on January 14, 1945. *AFM*

SAD SACK, a P-51 (code LC-A, s/n 44-14822) piloted by Maj. Merle J. Gilbertson of the 77th Fighter Squadron, 20th Fighter Group. Gilbertson is credited with 2.833 aerial victories and damaging one Do 217. *Olmstead*

Lil Jughaid, a P-51, (code KI-A, s/n 44-13790) piloted by Jum Burford of the 55th Fighter Squadron, 20th Fighter Group. *Jack Ilfrey*

Miss "(U)" Louise, a P-51D-5-NA (code MC-S, s/n 44–15049) piloted by Capt. Mel Ingebrightsen, pictured with Cpl. John Russell, S/Sgt. Harry Schuler and T/Sgt. Joseph Taylor, all of the 79th Fighter Squadron, 20th Fighter Group. *John Hudgens, via Jack Ilfrey*

O'SAGE CHIEF, a P-51D (code MC-J, s/n 44–13855) piloted by Capt. Harold O. Binkley, pictured with his crew chief, D. S. Miller, Sgt. Dancek, and armorer, Sgt. J.W. Hughes. Binkley is credited with destroying one Me 109 and one Fw 190. *Jack Ilfrey*

"Hells Belle", a P-51 (code MC-L, s/n 43–25054) piloted by Lt. Willard H. Lewis, Jr., of the 79th Fighter Squadron, 20th Fighter Group. He is pictured here with S/Sgt. Roy Robinson, T/Sgt. Ethan Schrader, and Sgt. Tony Kublin. Lewis damaged one Me 109. *Jack Ilfrey*

PRETTY BABY, a P-51C razorback (code MC-V, s/n 43–25064) piloted by 2nd Lt. James N. Reichard of the 79th Fighter Squadron, 20th Fighter Group. Reichard is credited with 0.5 aerial victories. *Jack Ilfrey*

BOB CAT V, a P-51D (code MC-T, s/n 44–13876) piloted by Lt. Col. Robert J. Meyer, CO of the 79th Fighter Squadron, 20th Fighter Group. Meyer destroyed three Fw 190s, damaging two Me 109s and one Fw 190, and a probable on a Me 410. *George Weymn, via Jack Ilfrey*

THE BUTCHER BOY, a P-51 (code LC-A, s/n 44–13378) piloted by 2nd Lt. Ted E. Slanker of the 77th Fighter Squadron, 20th Fighter Group. Slanker is credited with destroying one Fw 190 and damaging another. *Jack Ilfrey*

Miss Miami, a P-51D (code LC-F, s/n 44-14823) piloted by Lt. Reps D. Jones. Lt. Jones downed one Me 109, one Fw 190, damaged one Fw 190, and got a probable in this aircraft. Jones was in the 77th Fighter Squadron, 20th Fighter Group. *Jack Ilfrey*

PAT'S PONY, a P-51D (code LC-D, s/n 43-25042) piloted by Lt. Doug MacArthur of the 77th Fighter Squadron, 20th Fighter Group. Pictured with MacArthur are: Armorer Sgt. Cohen, Asst. Crew Chief Sgt. George Tomlinson and Crew Chief T/Sgt. Messier. *Jack Ilfrey*

"Berties Bet"/SHOOT YOU'RE FADED, a P-51 piloted by Robert Scott of the 79th Fighter Squadron, 20th Fighter Group. Shown with Scott is his crew chief Tex Schrader. *Jack Ilfrey*

THE FLYING DUTCHMAN, a P-51D shown with pilot Capt. Earl Hower of the 55th Fighter Squadron, 20th Fighter Group. *Jack Ilfrey*

IT'S THE KID, a P-51 piloted by Lt. Frederick H. Alexander of the 77th Fighter Squadron, 20th Fighter Group. Alexander is credited with two Me 109s destroyed. *Jack Ilfrey*

'JANEY GIRL' from Texas, a P-51 piloted by Capt. W. R. Yarbrough of the 20th Fighter Group. *MAFB*

California Cutie, a P–38 (code KI-S, s/n 42–67916) piloted by 1st Lt. Richard O. Loehnert of the 55th Fighter Squadron, 20th Fighter Group. Pictured with Loehnert is T/Sgt. Thomas Dickerson. Loehnert shot down two Me 109s on July 7, 1944. *Jack Ilfrey*

EZE DOES IT, a P–38J droopsnoot, piloted by Lt. Col. Harold Rau, CO of the 20th Fighter Group and bombadier Ezell. The droopsnoot had a bombadier compartment built into the nose, and would be the lead ship on level bombing missions. *Jack Ilfrey*

Strictly Stella's Baby, a P–38 piloted by Maj. Franklin, CO of the 79th Fighter Squadron, 20th Fighter Group. This P–38 is named in honor of Franklin's wife. Maj. Franklin holds the DFC as well as the Air Medal with three OLC. *MAFB*

A damaged P–38, piloted by Capt. Jack M. Ilfrey of the 79th Fighter Squadron, 20th Fighter Group. The damage happened when Capt. Ilfrey collided in mid-air with a German fighter over Berlin. *MAFB*

Wilda, a P–51D (s/n 44–14891, code LC-0) piloted by Maj. Merle B. Nichols. Nichols named this P–51 after his P–38. *Jack Ilfrey*

Gentle Annie, a P-38, (code MC-R, s/n 42-68166) piloted by Col. Harold J. Rau, 20th Fighter Group. This picture shows Col. Cy Wilson and Col. Harold J. Rau. Col. Rau destroyed five Nazi planes, including four on the ground. *OASM*

Snafuperman, a P-38J, pictured with Lockheed Test Pilot Tony LeVier—one of the finest test pilots to arrive overseas during the war. He performed unbelievable aerial demonstrations in the P-38. He even flew on one engine at tree top level while inverted. *Jack Ilfrey*

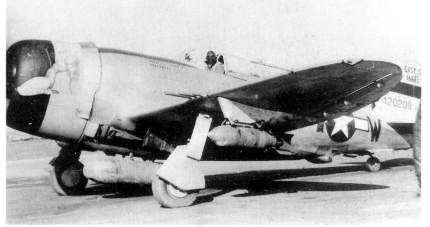

Jeanie, a P-47N (code 7U-W, s/n 420209) piloted by Maj. Weeger, CO of the 23rd Fighter Squadron, 36th Fighter Group, 9th Air Force. Note the name "Easy's Angels" on the tail. "Easy" was their former CO, Maj. "Easy" Miles, shot down January 22, 1945. *Delaney, via Crow*

ARKANSAS TRAVELER, a P-47 of the 36th Fighter Group, shown with Mr. Hart Miller, Vice President of Republic Aviation Corporation, and Col. Paul Douglas. *MAFB*

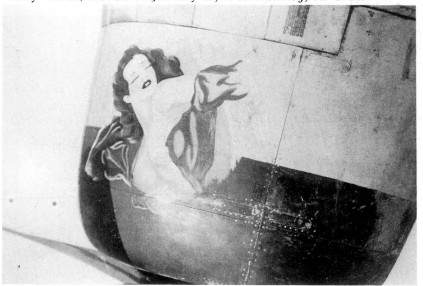

This P-47 was assigned to the 313th Fighter Squadron, 50th Fighter Group, 9th Air Force. Photo taken in France, 1945. *Kirk, via Crow*

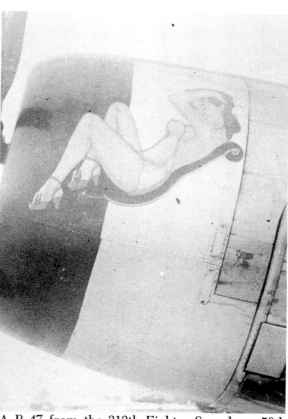

This P-47 was assigned to the 313th Fighter Squadron, 50th Fighter Group. *Kirk, via Crow*

A P-47 from the 313th Fighter Squadron, 50th Fighter Group. *Kirk, via Crow*

A P-47 from the 313th Fighter Squadron, 50th Fighter Group. *Kirk, via Crow*

A P-47 from the 313th Fighter Squadron, 50th Fighter Group. *Kirk, via Crow*

Another pinup on a P-47 from the 313th Fighter Squadron, 50th Fighter Group. *Kirk, via Crow*

The P-47 piloted by Lt. Gilbert C. Burns of the 313th Fighter Squadron, 50th Fighter Group. Burns shot down a Me 110 on January 3, 1944. *Hurt, via Crow*

LUCKY WABBIT II, a P-51 of the 343rd Fighter Squadron, 55th Fighter Group, 8th Air Force. *T. R. Bennett, via Jeff Ethell*

Annette, a P-51K of the 38th Fighter Squadron, 55th Fighter Group. Photo taken in Kaufbeuren, Germany, 1945. *Gimler, via Crow*

Vivacious Vera, shown on a portion of door retrieved from the wreckage of a P-38 (code CY-L, s/n 42-67053), originally assigned to Lt. Gilbride. Gilbride named the ship after his wife. After Gilbride was MIA, the plane was reassigned to Lt. Goudelock. *Olmstead*

BAMBI, a P-38 (s/n 42-67962) piloted by Lt. John Loren Odegard of the 338th Fighter Squadron, 55th Fighter Group. Odegard damaged a Me 110 on February 10, 1944, over Brunswick, Germany. *Donnie Watts*

Texas Ranger, a P-38 piloted by Lt. Col. Jack S. Jenkins of the 343rd Fighter Squadron, 55th Fighter Group. From left to right are Capt. Cureton, Capt. Leinweber, Professor Dobie (University of Texas), Lt. Jenkins, Maj. Webb, and Sgt. Causey. *Jenkins, via Jack Ilfrey*

Pitter PAT, a P-38 piloted by Lt. K. J. Sorace of the 343rd Fighter Squadron, 55th Fighter Group. Notice the jacket patch with the 94th Fighter Squadron's "Hat in the Ring" insignia. *Mrs. D. Starbuck, via Jack Ilfrey*

This P-47 (code UN-O, s/n 41-6216) was the first assigned aircraft of pilot Wayne J. O'Conner of the 63rd Fighter Squadron, 56th Fighter Group. O'Conner scored 1.5 aerial victories. *Maxwell AFB*

Stalag Luft III/I Wanted Wings, a P-47 piloted by Lt. Albert P. Knafelz of the 62nd Fighter Squadron, 56th Fighter Group, 8th Air Force. Lt. Knafelz is credited with one aerial victory. *Donnie Watts*

The P-47 piloted by Lt. W. A. Van Able of the 63rd Fighter Squadron, 56th Fighter Group. Pictured with Don Itza, his crew chief. *AFM*

Rozzie Geth, a P-47 (s/n 42-75207, Code LM-C) piloted by Capt. Fred J. Christensen of the 62nd Fighter Squadron, 56th Fighter Group. He destroyed 21.5 German planes in the air—six in one mission. This aircraft was named after his girl friend Rosamond Gethro. *T. Ivey*

The P-47 *BIG BASTARD*, (s/n 42–26086), after it crashed on the runway of the 2nd Service Group, in Iceland, when its landing gear failed during a refueling stop. It was on its way to the 56th Fighter Group. *AFM*

Pappy, a P-47 of the 56th Fighter Group. The 56th Fighter Group had more fighter aces than any of our other fighter groups. It also had two of the top scoring aces in Gabreski and Johnson. It was the highest scoring fighter group, in aerial victories, in the 8th Air Force. *AFM*

Zemkes Wolfpack, a P-47, on display in Paris, France. This airplane honored the 56th Fighter Group for destroying over 1,000 enemy aircraft. *AFM*

HOLY JOE, the P-47 piloted by Lt. Joseph Egan, Jr., of the 63rd Fighter Squadron, 56th Fighter Group. Lt. Egan is credited with five aerial victories. *AFM*

This P-47 was piloted by 1st Lt. S. O. Stamps of the 63rd Fighter Squadron, 56th Fighter Group. Lt. Stamps is credited with 0.5 aerial victories. *AFM*

Col. Francis Gabreski with his ground crew, just after returning from a mission over France. Col. Gabreski, CO of the 61st Fighter Squadron, 56th Fighter Group, is the leading ace in the ETO, with twenty-eight German planes to his credit. *OASM*

Dottie Dee 11, the P–47 piloted by 2nd Lt. Charles T. McBath of the 63rd Fighter Squadron, 56th Fighter Group. P. C. Dawson is shown standing in front of McBath's plane, Boxted, England. Dawson bears a striking resemblance to "Lt. Wolf" on the nose of this P–47. *Crow*

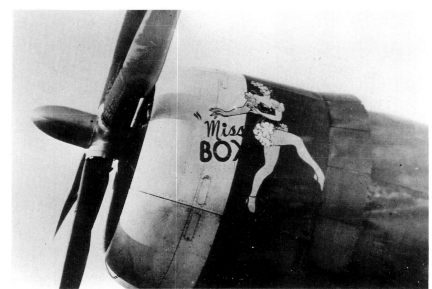

"Miss BOX", a P–47 from the 62nd Fighter Squadron, 56th Fighter Group. Photo taken at Raydonwood Airfield, November 1943. *Olmstead*

Li'l Goody, the P–47 piloted by Capt. Goodfleisch of the 56th Fighter Group. A young English lad is getting a hands-on tour of this jug's powerplant. His only remark was that "something isn't quite right." Photo taken October 16, 1943. *Olmstead*

CATEGORY "E", a P–47 "Double Bolt" (two seater P–47) of the 63rd Fighter Squadron, 56th Fighter Group. This two seater was used for attempted airborne radar interception over Germany. *McBeth, via Crow*

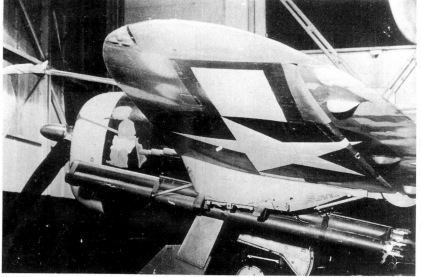

A rocket-armed P–47 of the 56th Fighter Group. *AFM*

"Bunky", a P–47 of the 56th Fighter Group. *AFM*

Princess Pat, a P–47, of the 63rd Fighter Squadron, 56th Fighter Group. *AFM*

A P–47 of the 63rd Fighter Squadron, 56th Fighter Group. The pilot, Lt. John H. "Lucky" Truluck, is credited with seven aerial victories and three others damaged in combat. The plane is UN:L, s/n 42–74750. "Lucky" is pictured, here, with his ground crew. *MAFB*

SLUGGER, the P–47 piloted by Lt. Norman E. Brooks of the 61st Fighter Squadron, 56th Fighter Group. Lt. Brooks is credited with two aerial victories. *AFM*

Miss Fire, a P–47 piloted by Capt. Fred Christensen of the 62nd Fighter Squadron, 56th Fighter Group. *OASM*

QUAKER SCHIEMEIL the P–47 piloted by 1st Lt. Walter R. Fredrick of the 63rd Fighter Squadron, 56th Fighter Group. Lt. Fredrick is credited with 0.5 aerial victories. *AFM*

"FATS" Btfsplk, a P-47 piloted by Lt. Stanley B. Morrill of the 62nd Fighter Squadron, 56th Fighter Group, featuring another of the "Lil' Abner" characters popular with the 56th Fighter Group. Morrill scored nine aerial victories. *T. Ivey*

JESSIE-O, a P-47 piloted by Capt. Eugene W. O'Neill, Jr. of the 62nd Fighter Squadron, 56th Fighter Group. This Irishman has a shamrock on his plane for good luck. O'Neill scored 4.5 aerial victories. *T. Ivey*

SNEAKY McGEE, a P-47 of the 56th Fighter Group. The 56th began fighting with the P-47 and continued throughout the war in it. *AFM*

DOC, the P-47 piloted by Capt. Donald D. Renwick of the 61st Fighter Squadron, 56th Fighter Group. Capt. Renwick is credited with one aerial victory. *AFM*

This P-47 flew with the 56th Fighter Group. *AFM*

G.O.P., a P-47 of the 56th Fighter Group. The pilot was obviously a Republican. *AFM*

Half Pint, a P–47 (code HV-P) piloted by Robert S. Johnson of the 61st Fighter Squadron, 56th Fighter Group. The painting is Pappy Yokum in his best jacket and hat. *Bill Hess*

Penrod and Sam, another P–47 (code LM-Q, s/n 42–25512) piloted by Robert S. Johnson. Penrod was the name of Johnson's crew chief and the name Sam came from Johnson's middle name. *B. Hess*

THE BEAST, a P–51 piloted by Lt. Geddis of the 111th Tactical Reconnaissance Squadron, 64th Fighter Wing. Geddis was killed in action in this aircraft. Picture taken in Dijon, France, 1944.

OKIE, a P–47D piloted by Maj. Quincy L. Brown of the 84th Fighter Squadron, 78th Fighter Group. Brown is credited with 12.33 aerial victories. He was later shot down by flak, and though he survived a belly landing, he was captured and killed by an SS Officer. *AFM*

No Guts-No Glory, a P–47 (code WZ-O) piloted by Maj. Ben I. Mayo Jr. of the 84th Fighter Squadron, 78th Fighter Group. Mayo is credited with four aerial victories. *MAFB*

Unmentionable, a P–47 (code WZ-B) piloted by Capt. John D. Irvin of the 84th Fighter Squadron, 78th Fighter Group. Capt. Irvin is credited with destroying two Me 109s, two Fw 190s and damaging one Fw 190. All were in *Unmentionable* except the last Me 109. *AFM*

Bad Medicine II, a P–47 (code WZ-X) piloted by Capt. Harold E. Stump of the 84th Fighter Squadron, 78th Fighter Group. Stump shot down an Me 109 on September 27, 1943. *AFM*

IRON ASS, a P–47 (code MX-X, s/n 44–19566) piloted by Maj. Jack J. Oberhansly of the 82nd Fighter Squadron, 78th Fighter Group. Oberhansly is credited with six aircraft destroyed, two probables, and one damaged. *AFM*

ROCKET JO, a P–47 (code MX-D) piloted by Capt. Robert E. Adamina of the 82nd Fighter Squadron, 78th Fighter Group. Adamina destroyed an Fw 190 on May 14, 1943. *AFM*

"*Roger the Lodger*", a P–47 piloted by Capt. Gerald E. Budd of the 84th Fighter Squadron, 78th Fighter Group, showing the checkered cowling that was painted on all three squadrons in the Group. *Crow*

Mud Creeker, a P–47 piloted by Lt. Dixie G. Jackson of the 82nd Fighter Squadron, 78th Fighter Group. Jackson began the war as a member of the RAF Eagle Squadron—scoring 7 kills. He was shot down over France on July 14, 1943. *L. Jackson*

Jeanie -V.O.S.-, a P–47D (code MX-E, s/n 42–8530) piloted by Lt. Warren M. Wesson of the 82nd Fighter Squadron, 78th Fighter Group. T/Sgt. Clarence H. Koskela is shown painting on a swastika to mark Wesson's sixth victory. *AFM*

Hun Hopper, a P–47 piloted by Lt. A. C. Dunken, of the 78th Fighter Group. Dunken is pictured here, with his crew chief, S/Sgt. Burnevik. *AFM*

Jr., a P–47 of the 78th Fighter Group. *AFM*

A P–47 of the 78th Fighter Group. *AFM*

A P–47 piloted by Lt. J. S. Sandmeier of the 78th Fighter Group. *AFM*

Vee Gail, a P–47 of the 78th Fighter Group assigned to Capt. R. E. Eby. In the cockpit is Bob Hope with his long time actress friend Francis Langford. *B. Hess*

"*Lee D.*," a P-51D (code WZ-H, s/n 44–63632) piloted by 1st Lt. William J. DeGain of the 84th Fighter Squadron, 78th Fighter Group. Lt. DeGain shot down an Me 109 on January 14, 1945, and an Fw 190 on March 19, 1945. Note the artwork under the name plate. *AFM*

Big Beautiful Doll, a P–51 piloted by Lt. Col. John D. Landers, CO of the 78th Fighter Group. Lander's P–51 was natural metal with black and white checks with red trim. The lettering was outlined in red setting off nicely the Japanese and German victory flags marking Landers' 14.5 aerial victories. *AFM*

Snootie Little Cutie, a P–51D of the 84th Fighter Squadron, 78th Fighter Group. *Olmstead*

BOB KAT, a P–47 piloted by 1st Lt. Archie W. Hill of the 82nd Fighter Squadron, 78th Fighter Group. Hill damaged an Fw 190 and shared a kill on an Me 109. *AFM*

SMALL BOY HERE, a P–51 piloted by 2nd Lt. John A. Kirk, III, of the 83rd Fighter Squadron, 78th Fighter Group. Kirk scored four aerial victories—none of which were in this ill–fated aircraft. The damage was sustained in a landing accident. *AFM*

A P–47 (code WZ-H) piloted by Lt. John R. Bertrand of the 84th Fighter Squadron, 78th Fighter Group. Bertrand shot down a Fw 190 on July 30, 1943. His crew chief was S/Sgt. R. N. Fitzpatrick. *AFM*

THE JOKER, a P–47 pictured with ground crewman Gilbert Hurt of the 86th Fighter Group, 525th Fighter Squadron, 12th Air Force. *Hurt, via Crow*

MISS DALLAS, a P–47D of the 525th Fighter Squadron, 86th Fighter Group. *Hurt, via Crow*

MISS TEXAS, a P–47 of the 525th Fighter Squadron, 86th Fighter Group. *Hurt, via Crow*

TOUCHE!, a P–47 of the 525th Fighter Squadron, 86th Fighter Group. *Hurt, via Crow*

SACK TIME SHIRLEY, a P–47 piloted by Lt. Willard Smith of the 525th Fighter Squadron, 86th Fighter Group. *Hurt, via Crow*

Miss Tennessee, a P–47D of the 525th Fighter Squadron, 86th Fighter Group. *Hurt, via Crow*

"*Sally*", a P–51B, got her nose bent a touch when she flew in too low on a strafing mission over a German airfield. *AFM*

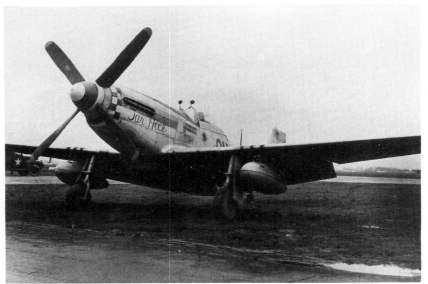

Tar Heel, a P–51 piloted by Capt. Kirke B. Everson of the 504th Fighter Squadron, 339th Fighter Group, 8th Air Force. Everson is credited with eleven aerial victories. *AFM*

StrawBoss 2, a P–51D (code PE-X, s/n 44–14111) piloted by Col. James D. Mayden, CO of the 352nd Fighter Group 8th Air Force. Col. Mayden (second from left), is pictured with his ground crew, based at Bodney, England. Col. Mayden scored two aerial victories. *AFM*

Cripes A'MIGHTY, a P–47 was the first of four aircraft named *Cripes A'Mighty* flown by Maj. George Preddy and was flown until April 1944. *Cripes A'Mighty 2nd* was flown until July 1944. *Cripes A'Mighty 3rd* was flown until August 1944. *ASM*

CRIPES A'MIGHTY 3RD, a P–51D, piloted by Maj. George Preddy of the 487th Fighter Squadron, 352nd Fighter Group. On Christmas Day, 1944, he was killed by Allied anti-aircraft fire. He was credited with 26.83 aerial victories, including two Me 109s on his last mission. *J. Moses*

A later photo of *Cripes A'Mighty 3rd*—with a few more victory crosses on its nose. Also shown are the ground crew that helped keep it in the air: S/Sgt. Lew Lunn, Crew Chief; Cpl. Red McVay, Asst.; and Sgt. M. G. Kuhaneck, Armorer. *USAF*

Sweetie FACE, a P–51 piloted by 1st Lt. Sheldon L. Heyer of the 487th Fighter Squadron, 352nd Fighter Group. *J. Moses*

PETIE 2nd, a P–51D (code HO-M, s/n 44–15151) also piloted by John C. Meyer (now a Lt. Col.). Meyer scored a total of twenty-four destroyed, one probable and one damaged. *J. Moses*

"Bonnie Lee", a P–47 of the 352nd Fighter Group. Note the dog. *AFM*

The Syracusan, a P–47 of the 486th Fighter Squadron, 352nd Fighter Group, piloted by Capt. Henry J. Miklajcyk, who has 7.5 aerial victories to his credit. Note the skull hidden in clouds between lightning bolts. *T. Ivey*

GIG'S-UP, a P-47 piloted by Maj. Edward J. Gignac of the 486th Fighter Squadron, 352nd Fighter Group. *AFM*

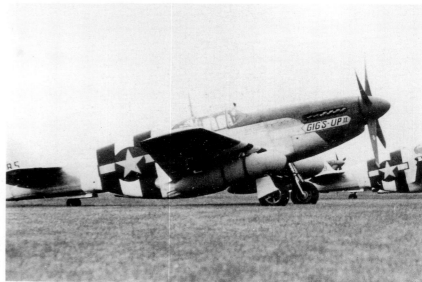

After the 486th converted to flying the P-51 Mustang, Maj. Gignac named his *GIG'S-UP II*. Gignac is credited with 1.5 aerial victories. *AFM*

RED RAIDER, a P-47 (code PE-W, s/n 42-2519) piloted by Lt. Fremont W. Miller of the 328th Fighter Squadron, 352nd Fighter Group. This aircraft carries a cowboy on a bucking bronco. *Mark Bacon*

HOT STUFF, a P-51B (code PZ-J) piloted by Lt. Col. Willie O. Jackson of the 486th Fighter Squadron, 352nd Fighter Group. Jackson is credited with seven aerial victories, one probable, and three damaged. *Donnie Watts*

THE WEST "by Gawd" VIRGINIAN/Jamie My Boy, a P-47 (code PE-X) assigned to the 328th Fighter Squadron of the 352nd Fighter Group. Piloted by Lt. Robert Powell, Jr. and Lt. Jamie Laring. The port side bears the name *Jamie My Boy*. *T. Ivey, via Powell*

The West "by Gawd" Virginian, a P-51 flown by Lt. Robert Powell, Jr. Powell carried the same nose art over from his P-47. *T. Ivey, via Powell*

LAMBIE, a P-47 (code HO-M, s/n 42-8529) piloted by Maj. John C. Meyer of the 487th Fighter Squadron, 352nd Fighter Group. Meyer scored 3.5 destroyed and one probable in this aircraft. Notice the Maltese Cross type victory markings. *J. Moses*

THIS IS IT!, a P-51 (code PZ-M, s/n 42-106609) piloted by Col. Joe L. Mason of the 486th Fighter Squadron, 352nd Fighter Group. Mason is credited with three Me 109s and 2 Fw 190s destroyed and damaging one Fw 190 and one Me 109. *Donnie Watts*

WILLIAM'S VILLIAN, a P-51 (code HO-B, s/n 43-6751) piloted by 1st Lt. Harry H. Barnes of the 487th Fighter Squadron, 352nd Fighter Group. Barnes is credited with 2.5 aerial victories and two damaged, all were Me 109s. *Tinker*

A closeup of *PETIE 2nd* and pilot, Lt. Col. John C. Meyer. *AFM*

Princess ELIZABETH, a P-51 (code HO-W) piloted by Capt. William T. Whisner of the 487th Fighter Squadron, 352nd Fighter Group. Whisner is credited with 15.5 aerial victories and two probables.

Miss Lace, a P–51 of the 486th Fighter Squadron, 352nd Fighter Group.

IT'S SUPER MOUSE, a P–51 (code PE-Z) of the 328th Fighter Squadron, 352nd Fighter Group. *Mark Bacon*

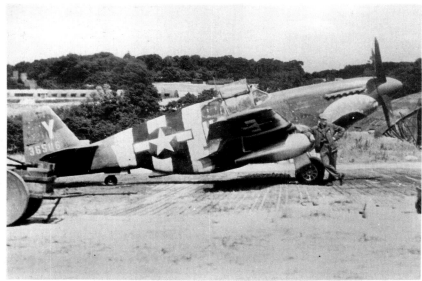

A rare shark-mouthed P–51 (code HO-V, s/n 43–6506), piloted by 1st Lt. Guy P. Taylor of the 487th Fighter Squadron, 352nd Fighter Group. Taylor shot down one Me 109 south of Hamburg.

Dove of Peace, a P–47D (code LH-X, s/n 42–25506) piloted by Col. Glenn Duncan, CO of the 353rd Fighter Group, 8th Air Force. Col. Duncan is credited with 19.5 aerial victories, all while flying P–47s. Sixteen victory swastikas are marked on this ship. *Crow*

SNEEZY, a P–47 of the 352nd Fighter Group.

Dove of Peace, after bellying-in to a Dutch field on July 7, 1944. Duncan's command was interrupted when *Dove of Peace* was downed by flak. Evading capture, he worked with the Dutch underground until advancing Allied forces helped return him to England. *M. Bacon*

When the 353rd Fighter Group transitioned to Mustangs, in April 1945, Col. Duncan kept the name *Dove of Peace* for his P–51. *AFM*

Arkansas Traveler, a P-47 (code LH-O) piloted by Capt. Dewey E. Newhart of the 350th Fighter Squadron, 353rd Fighter Group. Capt. Newhart has to his credit three aerial victories. Notice the black and white invasion stripes. *OASM*

"Dallas Doll", a P-51 (code SX-I, s/n 44–14495) piloted by 1st Lt. Frank H. Bouldin of the 352nd Fighter Squadron, 353rd Fighter Group. He is credited with three aerial victories. *MAFB*

ALABAMA RAMMER JAMMER, a P-51 piloted by 1st Lt. Arthur C. Cundy of the 352nd Fighter Squadron, 353rd Fighter Group. Cundy is credited with six aerial victories. *MAFB*

Maggie IV, a P-51 piloted by Lt. Kenneth "Choo Choo" Chetwood of the 350th Fighter Squadron, 353rd Fighter Group. Chetwood, was, at one time, the leading 8th Air Force loco-buster. He crash landed twice and bailed out once, and is credited with one aerial victory. *MAFB*

Prudence, a P–47 piloted by Capt. William F. Tanner of the 350th Fighter Squadron, 353rd Fighter Group. Capt. Tanner is credited with 5.5 aerial victories. *AFM*

Patricia Baby, a P–47 being loaded with bombs. The ground crewmen of the 353rd Fighter Group like other ground crews, were greatly appreciated by the pilots. These men are using the combination of caution, speed, and care in transferring the bomb to a bomb-lift cradle. *MAFB*

Smoocher, a wrecked P–47, of the 351st Fighter Squadron, 353rd Fighter Group. The 353rd perfected dive-bombing and ground attack techniques that were later adopted by the other P–47 units of the Eighth and Ninth Air Force. *AFM, via Crow*

A P–47D piloted by Lt. Col. Wayne K. Blickenstaff of the 350th Fighter Squadron, 353rd Fighter Group. Later, while flying P–51s, he shot down four Fw 190s on November 27, 1944, one Me 262 on February 22, 1945, and three Fw 190s plus two Me 109s on March 24, 1945. *Wright, via Crow*

Mud N'Mules, a P–47 (code LH-Q, s/n 42–76141) piloted by Capt. Dewey E. Newhart of the 350th Fighter Squadron, 353rd Fighter Group. Newhart is credited with three aerial victories. *Wright, via Crow*

Lucky 7, a P–47D piloted by Lt. L. Avakian of the 353rd Fighter Group. This aircraft was nicknamed *The Mole* (inscribed into checkerboarding on cowl). Notice the Maltese crosses banding the firewall. *AFM*

RAT A DAT, a P–47 (code LH-Q, s/n 42–26634) piloted by Capt. F. Saltree of the 350th Fighter Squadron, 353rd Fighter Group. *AFM*

Chief Wahoo, a P–47 (code YJ-L, s/n 42–7906) piloted by Maj. Frederick H. LeFebre of the 351st Fighter Squadron, 353rd Fighter Group. While flying this P–47, Le Febre is credited with 1.5 aerial victories. *AFM*

Margaret 3rd, a P–51 piloted by Maj. Walker L. "Dan'l" Boone of the 350th Fighter Squadron 353rd Fighter Group. Boone, in this Mustang, strafed nine enemy aircraft into junk in a single mission to run his score up to fifteen ground victories and two aerial victories. *MAFB*

MARTY, a P–47 (code YJ-L, s/n 42–22469) piloted by 1st Lt. Jack Terzian of the 351st Fighter Squadron, 353rd Fighter Group. Terzian shared a kill on an Fw 190 on March 6, 1944, with Maj. Vic L. Byers, Jr., also of the 351st Fighter Squadron. *Crow*

SHORT-FUSE SALLEE, a P–51D (code AJ-T, s/n 43–12434) piloted by Maj. Richard Turner of the 356th Fighter Squadron, 354th Fighter Group. He was the leading fighter ace of the Ninth Air Force. *OASM*

"SHORT-FUSE" another P-51 piloted by Lt. Col. Richard E. Turner of the 356th Fighter Squadron, 354th Fighter Group, 9th Air Force. Sallee had, by this time, married someone else, so the name was shortened to SHORT-FUSE. *B. Hess*

UNO-WHO? a P-51 piloted by Maj. George "Max" Lamb of the 356th Fighter Squadron, 354th Fighter Group. Lamb is credited with 7.5 aerial victories—all in P-51s. Under the name is a black mask much like that worn by Zorro or the Lone Ranger. *B. Hess*

"Grim Reaper", a P-51 (code GQ-U) piloted by Maj. Lowell K. Brueland of the 355th Fighter Squadron, 354th Fighter Group. Brueland is credited with 12.5 aerial victories. Notice the cloaked figure, ready to harvest. *B. Hess*

KILLER, a P-51B (code GQ-S) piloted by Maj. Robert W. Stephens of the 355th Fighter Squadron, 354th Fighter Group. Maj. Stephens is credited with thirteen aerial victories. *AFM*

KILLER! a P-51D piloted by Maj. Robert W. Stephens. Stephens named his new P-51D KILLER! after his P-51B, but added an ace of spades. *T. Ivey*

A P-47D, (code FT-L, s/n 44-20473) piloted by Maj. G. T. Eagleston of the 353rd Fighter Squadron, 354th Fighter Group. Maj. Eagleston is credited with 18.5 aerial victories. *AFM*

"KRIS-BEE", a P–47 of the 354th Fighter Group. This bumble bee is wearing goggles and carrying a bomb and has a machine gun in place of his stinger. *T. Ivey*

DING HAO, a P–51B piloted by Col. James H. Howard of the 356th Fighter Squadron, 354th Fighter Group. Col. Howard destroyed 13.33 enemy aircraft (7.33 with the AVG) and received the Congressional Medal of Honor. *B. Hess*

Another P–51 piloted by Maj. Eagleston. The eagle is the same, but the plane shows a different pattern of swastikas. Note the half-swastika. *Crow*

SQUAW-TOWN SQUASHER, a P–47 of the 354th Fighter Group. This robust American Indian carries a large club to make sure she always gets her man. Note the stars around the rim of the cowling. *T. Ivey*

JANE VII, a P–51 (code WR-B, s/n 44–72953) piloted by Maj. Bert W. Marshall, Jr. of the 354th Fighter Squadron, 355th Fighter Group. Maj. Marshall is credited with seven aerial victories. *Jane VII* is one among many P–51s piloted by Marshall named *Jane*. MAFB

Texas Terror IV, a P–51 (code WR-X, s/n 44–13571) piloted by 1st Lt. Lee G. Mendenhall of the 354th Fighter Squadron, 355th Fighter Group. Lt. Mendenhall is credited with 0.5 aerial victories. *AFM*

Ann Anita/Alabama Bound, a P–51 (code WR-M, s/n 42–1064) piloted by Lt. Duran Vickery of the 354th Fighter Squadron, 355th Fighter Group. *Jeff Ethell*

JAKE THE SNAKE, a P–51 of the 358th Fighter Squadron, 355th Fighter Group. *Jeff Ethell*

A P–47 piloted by 1st Lt. Leslie D. Minchew of the 354th Fighter Squadron, 355th Fighter Group, until his transfer to the 357th Fighter Squadron. Lt. Minchew, later promoted to Captain, is credited with 5.5 aerial victories. *AFM*

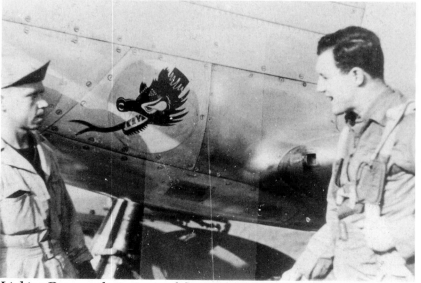

Licking Dragon, the insignia of the 357th Fighter Squadron, 355th Fighter Group. Standing by the P–51 is the squadron CO, Maj. John Elder and the crew chief, Billy Mitchell. Maj. Elder scored eight aerial victories and one damaged. *AFM*

Lil Jo/Speed, a P–47, (code WR-P, s/n 42–8404) piloted by "Speed" Hubbard, 354th Fighter Squadron, 355th Fighter Group, 8th Air Force. *Lil Jo* was shot down by flak November 13, 1943. Hubbard evaded capture and returned to the group in June of 1944. *Crow*

NAZI HOT FOOT, a P–51 of the 359th Fighter Squadron, 356th Fighter Group. *AFM*

STARDUSTER, a P–51 of the 359th Fighter Squadron, 356th Fighter Group. *AFM*

"KOYLI RENEE", a P–51D-15 piloted by 1st Lt. Glenn Crum of the 359th Fighter Squadron, 356th Fighter Group. Crum damaged an Me 109 on November 27, 1944, while flying this aircraft. *AFM*

GEORGIA'S BEST, a P–47, s/n 42-26239, piloted by 1st Lt. Durward B. Mercer of the 360th Fighter Squadron, 356th Fighter Group. Mercer is credited with destroying one Fw 190 and damaging another. *AFM*

JERSEY JERK, a P–51 (code QI-T, s/n 44–15152) piloted by Maj. Donald Jackson Strait of the 361st Fighter Squadron, 356th Fighter Group. Strait is credited with 13.5 aerial victories. Also flying in this formation is *JETT JOB* and others of the 361st Squadron. *AFM*

Lady Doris, a P–51 of the 360th Fighter Squadron, 356th Fighter Group. *Crow*

Little Bitch, a P–51 piloted by Capt. Dave T. Perron of the 362nd Fighter Squadron, 357th Fighter Group. Capt. Perron is credited with three aerial victories. *Jeff Ethell*

Muddy, a P–51, (code G4–K, s/n 44–11697) piloted by 2nd Lt. James A. Gasser of the 362nd Fighter Squadron, 357th Fighter Group. Lt. Gasser is credited with one aerial victory. *Olmstead, via Ethell*

Passion WAGON, a P–51D (code G4–A, s/n 13691) piloted by 1st Lt. Arval J. Roberson of the 362nd Fighter Squadron, 357th Fighter Group. Roberson scored six aerial victories. The aircraft was later transferred to the 364th Fighter Squadron. *Jeff Ethell*

A P–51D (code G4–A, s/n 44–72199) piloted by Capt. Charles E. Weaver of the 362nd Fighter Squadron, 357th Fighter Group. Pictured on the right is Capt. Weaver and on the left is S/Sgt. Lybarger. Weaver is credited with eight aerial victories. *Olmstead*

Another picture of Capt. Weaver's P–51, with Frank Hurbis, the 362nd's mailman. Note the elaborate kill marks on this plane. *Crow*

THE SHILLELAGH, a P–51 piloted by Lt. Col. John A. Storch of the 364th Fighter Squadron, 357th Fighter Group. Storch is credited with 10.5 aerial victories. *Olmstead*

U'VE HAD IT!, a P–51B (code G4–H, s/n 42–106452) piloted by Maj. John B. England of the 362nd Fighter Squadron, 357th Fighter Group. Maj. England is credited with 17.5 aerial victories. *Olmstead*

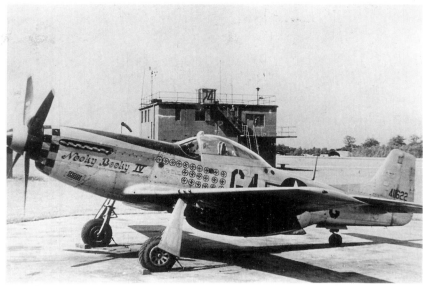

Nooky Booky IV, a P–51K (code G4–C, s/n 44–11622) piloted by Maj. Leonard "Kit" Carson of the 362nd Fighter Squadron, 357th Fighter Group. Carson is credited with 18.5 aerial victories. *Olmstead*

LITTLE SHRIMP, a P–51D (code B6–V) piloted by Maj. Robert W. Foy of the 363rd Fighter Squadron, 357th Fighter Group. Foy is credited with fifteen aerial victories. *Olmstead*

CHICAGO GUN MOLL, a P–51B piloted by 1st Lt. Robert D. Brown of the 362nd Fighter Squadron, 357th Fighter Group. Brown is credited with two aerial victories. *Olmstead*

DESERT RAT, a P–51D (code B6–B, s/n 44–13714) piloted by 1st Lt. Hershel T. Pascoe of the 363rd Fighter Squadron, 357th Fighter Group. Pascoe is credited with one aerial victory. *Olmstead*

BERLIN EXPRESS, a P–51C (s/n 42–103309) piloted by 1st Lt. William B. Overstreet of the 363rd Fighter Squadron, 357th Fighter Group. Overstreet is credited with 2.25 aerial victories. *Olmstead*

HORSES ITCH, a P-51D (code B6-D, s/n 44–13518) piloted by Maj. Edwin W. Hiro of the 363rd Fighter Squadron, 357th Fighter Group. Although the nose looks white here, it is in the 357th's red and yellow. Hiro scored five aerial victories. *Olmstead*

MOUNTAINEER, a P-51D piloted by 1st Lt. Paul N. Bowles of the 363rd Fighter Squadron, 357th Fighter Group. Bowles is credited with one aerial victory on April 19, 1945, when he shot down an Me 262. *Olmstead*

Moose, a P-51D-20-NA (code G4-S, s/n 44–63221) piloted by Lt. M. A. "Moose" Becraft of the 362nd Fighter Squadron, 357th Fighter Group. Becraft is credited with one aerial victory. There are also six swastikas for ground victories. *Olmstead*

Texas Ranger, a P-51 (code G4-E, s/n 43–6698) piloted by Lt. Otto D. Jenkins of the 362nd Fighter Squadron, 357th Fighter Group. Jenkins is credited with 8.5 aerial victories. *Olmstead*

Little Joe, a P-51D (code B6-B, s/n 44–13887) piloted by Lt. Joe Cannon of the 363rd Fighter Squadron, 357th Fighter Group. Cannon was credited with damaging an Me 262 on March 19, 1945. *Olmstead*

BIG MAC Junior, a P-51 piloted by Capt. John R. Brown of the 364th Fighter Squadron, 357th Fighter Group. Brown damaged an Fw 190 on July 12, 1944. Note the eye and stylized shark mouth. *T. Ivey*

HURRY HOME HONEY, a P-51D-15-NA, (code C5-T, s/n 44-14868) piloted by Capt. Richard A. Peterson of the 364th Fighter Squadron, 357th Fighter Group. Peterson is credited with 15.5 aerial victories, one probable, and two damaged. *Olmstead*

Hurry Home Honey, a P-51 (code C5-T, s/n 44-13586), the second of Capt. Richard A. Peterson's P-51s, all named *Hurry Home Honey*, named for the way his wife ended all of her letters to him. *MAFB*

$ BLACKPOOL BAT, a P-51 piloted by George George, 363rd Fighter Squadron, 357th Fighter Group. George is sitting on the wing with his future bride, who is from Blackpool, Scotland. *Overstreet*

$ BLACKPOOL BAT takes wing. *via B. Hess/T. Ivie*

Shanty Irish, a P-51 (code G4-Q) piloted by Lt. Gilbert Mouzon O'Brien of the 362nd Fighter Squadron, 357th Fighter Group. O'Brien is credited with seven aerial victories, and 2.5 damaged. *Overstreet*

SHOO SHOO BABY, a P-51B-10-NA (code C5-L, s/n 42-106447) of the 364th Fighter Squadron, 357th Fighter Group. *Crow*

SPEEDBALL ALICE, a P–51B–5 (code B6–F, s/n 43–6933) piloted by Lt. Donald H. Bochkay of the 363rd Fighter Squadron, 357th Fighter Group. Bochkay is credited with 13.83 victories. The winged ace of clubs was the insignia used by a pre-war motorcycle racer. *Crow*

Marymae, a P–51 of the 362nd Fighter Squadron, 357th Fighter Group. *Crow*

LONESOME POLECAT, a P–51D–10–NA (code B6–H, s/n 44–14356) piloted by 1st Lt. Keehn Landis of the 363rd Fighter Squadron, 357th Fighter Group. The one victory marker on the aircraft was earned on September 18, 1944. The damage is from a taxiing accident. *Crow*

LOUISIANA HEAT WAVE, a P–51D flown by Lt. Crenshaw of the 369th Fighter Squadron, 357th Fighter Group. Lt. Crenshaw has seven aerial victories and one probable. *B. Hess*

Temptation, a P–51 piloted by Lt. Mathew Martin of the 362nd Fighter Squadron, 357th Fighter Group. Note the apple with a bite missing below the word "temptation". *Donnie Watts*

1st Lt. William B. Overstreet in this P–39 Airaco-bra, used for training exercises in Santa Rosa, California. Overstreet scored 2.25 aerial victories with the 363rd Fighter Squadron, 357th Fighter Group. *Overstreet*

Glamorus Glen, a P–51 piloted by Capt. Charles E. Yeager of the 363rd Fighter Squadron, 357th Fighter Group. This plane and others to follow were named for his wife Glennis. Yeager scored 10.5 aerial victories. *Overstreet*

GLAMOROUS GLEN III, a P–51D–15–NA (code B6–Y, s/n 44–14888)—another of the aircraft piloted by Yeager during his service in the 363rd Fighter Squadron. Yeager scored 10.5 aerial victories—five on October 12 and four more on November 27, 1944. *Crow*

The "Yokum Family", P–47s of one of the flights in the 368th Fighter Squadron, 359th Fighter Group, 8th Air Force. All of the planes were named after characters in the comic strip "Lil' Abner." *MAFB*

BIG DOG, a P–47 piloted by Lt. John L. Downing of the 359th Fighter Group, pictured with Crew Chief S/Sgt. Charles Boskin on March 27, 1944, just before the group converted from the P–47s to P–51s. *MAFB*

LOU IV, a P-51, (code E2-C, s/n 44-13410) piloted by Col. Thomas Christian of the 375th Fighter Squadron, 361st Fighter Group, 8th Air Force. Col. Christian was killed in action on August 12, 1944. *AFM*

Ferocious Frankie, a P-51D piloted by Lt. Col. Wallace E. Hopkins of the 361st Fighter Group. Hopkins is credited with four aerial victories—two on May 29, 1944, and two on August 8, 1944. *AFM*

EIGHT NIFTIES, a P-47 of the 361st Fighter Group. Photo taken at St. Dizier, France, 1945. *Gorskey, via Crow*

THE BEAST, a P-47 of the 361st Fighter Group. *Gorskey, via Crow*

Sweet Thing III, a P-47 shown with Lt. Col. Webb, CO of the 374th Fighter Squadron, 361st Fighter Group. Webb is credited with four aerial victories. *Gorskey, via Crow*

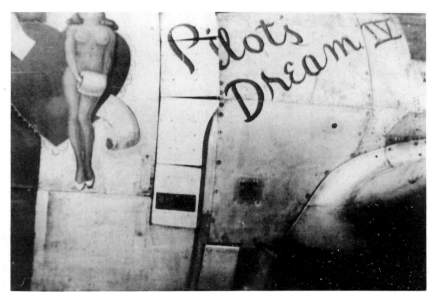

Miss CAESAR, THE "Greenpoint Gladiator", a P–47 of the 361st Fighter Group. *Gorskey, via Crow*

Pilot's Dream IV, a P–47 of the 361st Fighter Group. *Gorskey, via Crow*

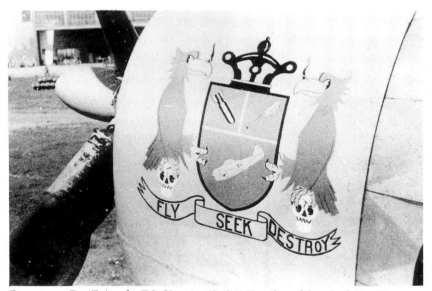

WHY PICK ON ME?!!, a P–47 (code B8–N, s/n 43–3522) piloted by Lt. Robert McCormack of the 379th Fighter Squadron, 362nd Fighter Group, 9th Air Force. *Marles, via Crow*

Bonnie, a P–47 (code B8–Y, s/n 42–0413) piloted by 2nd Lt. Eugene Martin, Jr. of the 379th Fighter Squadron, 362nd Fighter Group. The crest on the cowl carries the motto "Fly, Seek, Destroy". *Marles, via Crow*

JASPER, a P–47 of the 362nd Fighter Group. *Marles, via Crow*

A P–47 of the 362nd Fighter Group. *Marles, via Crow*

A P-47 of the 362nd Fighter Group. *Marles, via Crow*

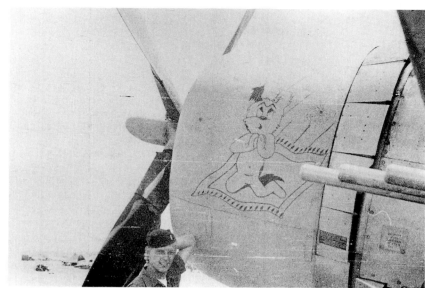

A P-47 of the 362nd Fighter Group. *Marles, via Crow*

LIL' IZZY, a P-47 of the 362nd Fighter Group. *Marles, via Crow*

FIVE BY FIVE, a P-47 piloted by CO Col. Joseph L. Laughlin, 379th Fighter Squadron, 362nd Fighter Group. Laughlin is credited with one aerial victory. *Marles, via Crow*

KAREN LEE, a P-47 of the 362nd Fighter Group. *Marles, via Crow*

CITY OF PARIS, a P-51 piloted by Maj. Robert McWherter of the 382nd Fighter Squadron, 363rd Fighter Group. McWherter is credited with one aerial victory while in the 17th Provisional Squadron, Southwest Pacific, and three while in the 363rd. *Donnie Watts*

HOO FLUNG DUNG, a P-51 (code C3–M, s/n 43–6438). This photo shows the opposite side of the *CITY OF PARIS.*" *Donnie Watts*

PRINCESS MARGE/*Gordoff's Baby*, a P-51 (code C3–L) piloted by Lt. Raymond E. Schillenef of the 382nd Fighter Squadron, 363rd Fighter Group. Schillenef scored one aerial victory. *Gordoff's Baby* is painted on the starboard side. *T. Ivey*

"*Look Homeward Angel II*", a P-51 piloted by Capt. Arthur B. McCormick Jr. of the 385th Fighter Squadron, 364th Fighter Group, 8th Air Force. Pictured left to right: Capt. Murphy, Maj. Crombie, Capt. Hargrove, Capt. McCormick, Capt. Fine and Lt. Houck. *C. Carter*

"*CASSIE'S Chassis*," a P-51 piloted by Lt. Manuel L. Casagrande of the 383rd Fighter Squadron, 364th Fighter Group. Casagrande shot down one Me 109. *C. Carter*

Jeanne II a P-51 piloted by Capt. Gerald Fine and *BOILERMAKER SPECIAL*, a P-51 piloted by Lt. Robert W. Boydston. Both planes have the 385th Squadron code 5E. *C. Carter*

PUNKIN II, a P-51 piloted by Lt. Robert S. Faulkner of the 384th Fighter Squadron, 364th Fighter Group. Pictured left to right are J. Hughes, Faulkner, H. Schwartz, D. Leftwich, B. Leavell, and P. Hahn on February 13, 1945, the day Faulkner finished his tour. *C. Carter*

The Smiling Shark, a P-51 flown by Lt. Edward Anderson. He explained, "It was supposed to be a tiger shark, but due to my poor artistry it appeared to be smiling." Sgt. H. Van Pelt is on the wing. *C. Carter*

Coffin Wit' Wings, a P-51D of the 385th Fighter Squadron, 364th Fighter Group. Note the damaged propellers. Photo taken in Honnington, England on October 13, 1944. *E. McDowell*

Esie 4, a P-51D of the 364th Fighter Group, 385th Fighter Squadron piloted by Maj. Carl W. Stapleton. Stapleton shot down a Fw 190 December 12, 1944. Photo taken at Honnington, England on December 20, 1944. *E. McDowell*

GROSS ARSCH VOGEL, a P-51 of the 364th Fighter Group, 385th Fighter Squadron, of the 67th Fighter Wing. Photo taken at Honnington, England on October 17, 1944. *E. McDowell*

Strellita III, a P-51 piloted by Lt. Curtis S. Maft of the 385th Fighter Squadron, 364th Fighter Group, pictured with his crew chief. Note this aircraft shows the checkered canopy bar also. *C. Carter*

HETTIE, a P–38J (s/n 42–88104) of the 384th Fighter Squadron, 364th Fighter Group. *C. Carter*

MY BEST BET II, a P–47 of the 365th Fighter Group. *Rothery, via Crow*

Slick Chick, a P–47 of the 365th Fighter Group. *Schaffer, via Crow*

COFFEY'S POT, a P–47D piloted by Lt. Col. Robert L. Coffee, Jr. of the 388th Fighter Squadron, 365th Fighter Group. Coffee is credited with destroying four Me 109s, a Fw 190, and a Ju 52. Picture taken on D-Day, 1944. *Ward, via Crow*

LIL OKIES, a P–47 of the 365th Fighter Group. *Rothery, via Crow*

PEGGY/PEG O' MY HEART, a P-47 of the 387th Fighter Squadron, 365th Fighter Group. *Rothery, via Crow*

PICCADILLY, a P-47 of the 387th Fighter Squadron, 365th Fighter Group. *Rothery, via Crow*

HAUL'IN ASS II, a P-47 of the 365th Fighter Group. *Rothery, via Crow*

PEGGY SHORT, a P-47 of the 365th Fighter Group. *Rothery, via Crow*

Mortician's Delight, a P-47 of the 365th Fighter Group. *Rothery, via Crow*

Screamin' Weemie, a P-47 piloted by Maj. Louis T. Houck of the 387th Fighter Squadron, 365th Fighter Group. *Rothery, via Crow*

OL' SMOKIE, a P-47 piloted by Capt. Andrew W. Smoak of the 387th Fighter Squadron, 365th Fighter Group. Lt. Smoak shared a kill on an Me 109 on September 11, 1944, and destroyed two Fw 190s on November 19, 1944. *Rothery, via Crow*

Sally Flat Foot III, a P-47 piloted by 1st Lt. William L. Ward of the 386th Fighter Squadron, 365th Fighter Group. Ward shot down one Me 109 and damaged another on June 22, 1944. He destroyed his second Me 109 on November 28, 1944. *Ward, via Crow*

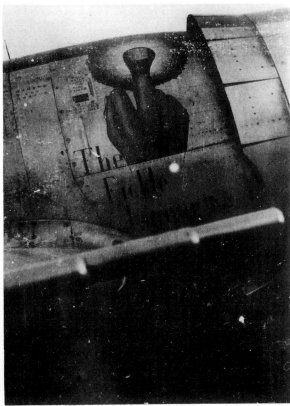

A close-up view of the art work on the cowl of *Sally Flat Foot III*. The ground crew for *Sally* consisted of Sgt. McDonough, Sgt. Slate, and Sgt. Freeman. *Ward, via Crow*

The Fickle Finger, a P-47 piloted by Maj. George R. Brooking of the 386th Fighter Squadron, 365th Fighter Group. Maj. Brooking is credited with one aerial victory. *Ward, via Crow*

Tessy, a P-47 of the 365th Fighter Group. *Schaffer, via Crow*

CORNY BABE, a P–47D, s/n 44–2043, of the 391st Fighter Squadron, 366th Fighter Group, 9th Air Force. Not only was this aircraft a loco-buster, but it also shows three tanks destroyed, top hats for top cover and brooms for fighter sweeps. *Crow*

My Bub, a P–47 of the 391st Fighter Squadron, 366th Fighter Group. Note the messages on the 500 pound bombs. The first being "Danger", the second, "To Adolph, best wishes". *Heimerl, via Crow*

A P–47 of the 390th Fighter Squadron, 366th Fighter Group. Photo taken in Belgium, 1945. *O'Malley, via Crow*

A P–47 of the 390th Fighter Squadron, 366th Fighter Group. Photo taken in Belgium, 1945. *O'Malley, via Crow*

Blondie, a P–47 piloted by 1st Lt. John T. Picton of the 390th Fighter Squadron, 336th Fighter Group. *Picton, via Crow*

HEARTLESS HELEN/PURDY SHARP, a P–47 piloted by Lt. Edward W. Purdy of the 389th Fighter Squadron, 366th Fighter Group. Purdy is credited with three aerial victories. *Hayes, via Crow*

74

FICKLE FLOSSY III, a P-47 of the 391st Fighter Squadron, 366th Fighter Group. *Heimerl, via Crow*

Peg O' My Heart, a P-47 assigned to Lt. Floyd N. Hass. Lt. Hass is credited with one confirmed aerial victory. In this photo, the pilot and crew chief inspect damage inflicted to the port wing. *AFM*

Lt. Sampson sitting in the cockpit of *Peg O' My Heart* after safely completing a belly landing in the damaged ship. *Donnie Watts*

"Butch II", a P-38 piloted by Capt. Horace M. Hartwig of the 392nd Fighter Squadron, 367th Fighter Group, 9th Air Force. Capt. Hartwig is credited with one aerial victory. *367th Fighter Group, via Jack Curtis*

Viking 2, a P-38 piloted by Jimmy Paschell of the 392nd Fighter Squadron, 367th Fighter Group. *367th Fighter Group, via Jack Curtis*

ARKANSAS TRAVELER, a P-38 piloted by 1st Lt. James O. Fincher of the 392nd Fighter Squadron, 367th Fighter Group. Lt. Fincher is credited with one aerial victory. *367th Fighter Group, via Jack Curtis*

"KOZY KOZA", a P–38 piloted by Lt. Sam Plotecia of the 392nd Fighter Squadron, 367th Fighter Group. *367th Fighter Group, via Jack Curtis*

"LITTLE BUCKAROO", a P–38 piloted by R. C. "Buck" Rogers of the 392nd Fighter Squadron, 367th Fighter Group. *367th Fighter Group, via Jack Curtis*

LUCKY IRISH, a P–38 piloted by Lt. Jerry O'Donnell of the 392nd Fighter Squadron, 367th Fighter Group. *367th Fighter Group, via Jack Curtis*

"*Philbert 3,*" a P–38 piloted by Maj. Mathison, CO of the 394th Squadron, 367th Fighter Group. Wilbur Siemsen and Ernie Snow are pictured with the plane. *367th Fighter Group, via Jack Curtis*

Curly Six, a P–38 piloted by Jack L. Reed of the 394th Fighter Squadron, 367th Fighter Group. *367th Fighter Group, via Jack Curtis.*

A damaged P–38 of the 394th Fighter Squadron, 367th Fighter Group after it was bellied-in at St. Dizier, France in 1944. Pilot of this aircraft was John Lund. *Crow*

DADDY RABBIT, a P-38 piloted by Lt. Robert E. Good of the 393rd Fighter Squadron, 367th Fighter Group. Lt. Good is credited with one aerial victory. *367th Fighter Group, via Jack Curtis*

Gung Ho, a P-38 piloted by Col. Edwin S. Chickering, CO of the 367th Fighter Group. *367th Fighter Group, via Jack Curtis*

Waterloo Belle, a P-38 piloted by Lt. William H. Lemley of the 394th Fighter Squadron, 367th Fighter Group. Lt. Lemley is credited with one aerial victory. *367th Fighter Group, via Jack Curtis*

Flaming Fury, a P-38 piloted by Bill Lewis of the 394th Fighter Squadron, 367th Fighter Group. *367th Fighter Group, via Jack Curtis*

TRAIL BLAZER, a P-38 droopsnoot piloted by Lt. Curtis of the 394th Fighter Squadron, 367th Fighter Group. *367th Fighter Group, via Jack Curtis*

TACOMAN, a P-38 piloted by Lt. Joseph A. Dobrowolski of the 393rd Fighter Squadron, 367th Fighter Group. Lt. Dobrowolski is credited with one aerial victory. *367th Fighter Group, via Jack Curtis*

"MAGGIE 2", a P–38 piloted by Gene Hinkley of the 394th Fighter Squadron, 367th Fighter Group. *367th Fighter Group, via Jack Curtis*

DUCK-BUTT, piloted by Arthur Witters of the 392nd Fighter Squadron, 367th Fighter Group. *367th Fighter Group, via Jack Curtis*

"STUPE", a P–47 of the 394th Fighter Squadron, 367th Fighter Group. *367th Fighter Group, via Jack Curtis*

A P–47 piloted by Dick Brennan of the 394th Fighter Squadron, 367th Fighter Group. *367th Fighter Group, via Jack Curtis*

REPUBLIC'S SPARE PARTS, a P–47 of 394th Fighter Squadron, 367th Fighter Group. *367th Fighter Group, via Jack Curtis*

JUST BESS, a P–47 piloted by 2nd Lt. Bruce Q. Baize of the 392nd Fighter Squadron, 367th Fighter Group, suffered damage when it hit a radar truck during landing. Baize is credited with two aerial victories. *367th Fighter Group, via Jack Curtis*

patty anne, a P–38 piloted by Charles Croker of the 394th Fighter Squadron, 367th Fighter Group. *367th Fighter Group, via Jack Curtis*

Penny, a P–47 piloted by Clark Egan of the 394th Fighter Squadron, 367th Fighter Group. *367th Fighter Group, via Jack Curtis*

Mom's Irish Mick, a P–47 of the 393rd Fighter Squadron, 367th Fighter Group. This plane bellied–in while still carrying its bombs. Photo taken at Eschborn, Germany. *367th Fighter Group, via Jack Curtis*

Hellzapoppin II, a P–38 piloted by Maj. Joseph H. Griffin. Griffin is pictured here with Sgt. James Griffin (his brother and crew chief). Griffin also flew a P–40 named *HELLZAPOPPIN* in the Pacific. He destroyed three Japanese and four German planes. *OASM*

Frigid Midget, a P–47 piloted by Lt. Jack H. Hallett of the 394th Fighter Squadron, 367th Fighter Group. Hallett is credited with one Me 109 on December 16, 1944. *Snow, via Crow*

The left cowl of *Poutin' Poot*. *Jack Curtis*

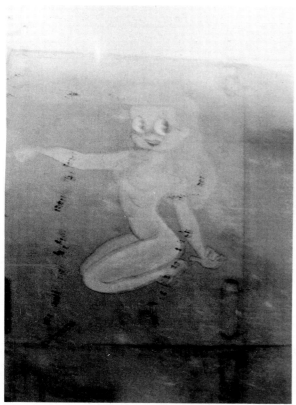

The right cowl of the P–47 *Poutin' Poot*, piloted by Jack Curtis of the 367th Fighter Group. *Jack Curtis*

Pootie Two, another P–47 piloted by Jack Curtis. Curtis is pictured here with Crew Chief Carl Lownes and Assistant Crew Chief Howard Bourquin. *367th Fighter Group, via Jack Curtis*

Royal Flush, a P–38 piloted by Henry Gillespie of the 392nd Fighter Squadron, 367th Fighter Group. *367th Fighter Group, via Jack Curtis*

Moonlight Cock-Tail, a P–38 piloted by Clark R. "Doc" Livingston of the 392nd Fighter Squadron, 367th Fighter Group. *367th Fighter Group, via Jack Curtis*

Buccaneer, a P–47 piloted by Lt. Edward F. Janesic of the 367th Fighter Group. *Edward Janesic*

Little Stinker, a P–47 of the 392nd Fighter Squadron, 367th Fighter Group. *367th Fighter Group, via Jack Curtis*

Slick Chick, a P-47 piloted by Col. Frank S. Perego, CO of the 368th Fighter Group, 9th Air Force. Pappy Pounds was the crew chief. *Marvin Rosvold*

MIL O MINE, a P-47 of the 395th Fighter Squadron, 368th Fighter Group. Photo taken at Nurnberg, Germany, May 1945. *Eklund, via Crow*

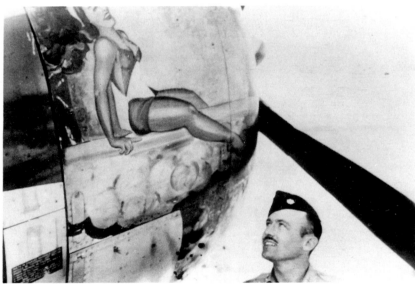

Luscious Lena, a P-47D piloted by Maj. Harold P. Sparks of the 396th Fighter Squadron, 368th Fighter Group. This is only one in a series of five different jugs to have this artwork. Sparks is credited with damaging an Fw 190 on July 7, 1944. *Marvin Rosvold*

RIDGE RUNNER, a P-47 piloted by Walter Johnson of the 368th Fighter Group. *Marvin Rosvold*

Rough AND Ready, a P-47 piloted by 1st Lt. William J. Garry of the 395th Fighter Squadron, 368th Fighter Group. Garry is credited with destroying two Me 109s and two Fw 190s. *Marvin Rosvold*

ICE COLD KATTIE, a P-47 of the 368th Fighter Group. *Marvin Rosvold*

Texas Terror, a P–47 of the 368th Fighter Group, pictured with ground crewmen (left to right) Rudy Mueller, Joe Scalzo and Al Aquino. *Marvin Rosvold*

A P–47 of the 368th Fighter Group with Cpl. Guenter. *Marvin Rosvold*

SLEEPY JEAN, a P–47 of the 395th Fighter Squadron, 368th Fighter Group. Pictured with the pilot, Lt. Bill Weyland, is Crew Chief Sgt. Mohn. *Marvin Rosvold*

THE OLD MAN, a P–47 piloted by Maj. Thomas J. Carbine, CO of the 397th Fighter Squadron, 368th Fighter Group. He is credited with 0.5 aerial victories. *Marvin Rosvold*

DRAGON LADY, a P–47 piloted by 2nd Lt. Paul R. Jasper of the 396th Fighter Squadron, 368th Fighter Group. Jasper shot down an Me 109 on June 22, 1944. *Marvin Rosvold*

82

Stud, a P-47 of the 368th Fighter Group. *Marvin Rosvold*

The Down Necker, a P-47, with ground crew, of the 368th Fighter Group. Pictured are Baland, Rilley, and Carpenter. *Marvin Rosvold*

Loopin Lou, a P-47 piloted by LeLoup of the 395th Fighter Squadron, 368th Fighter Group. *Marvin Rosvold*

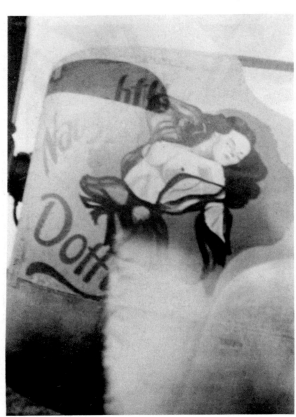

Naughty Dotty, a P-47 piloted by Steven Halpin of the 368th Fighter Group. *Marvin Rosvold*

ARIZONA LORRAINE, a P-47 (code C2-L, s/n 44-33250) piloted by Earl Kielgass of the 396th Fighter Squadron, 368th Fighter Group. *Marvin Rosvold*

PASSIONATE VIOLET, a P-47 piloted by Tommy Hoade of the 368th Fighter Group. *Marvin Rosvold*

MILLY K, a P-47 of the 368th Fighter Group.
Marvin Rosvold

Susie To Win, a P-47 of the 368th Fighter Group.
Marvin Rosvold

PRIDE OF MURPHY'S BOYS, a P-47 of the
368th Fighter Group.

LES VIN, LES FEMMES, ET LES CHANSONS, a P-38 piloted by Maj.
Slip of the 485th Fighter Squadron, 370th Fighter Group. Translates
"Wine, Women, and Song." P-38 National Association, via Joe Kuhn

Miss Appropriated, a P-51D found and made flyable at Orleans-Bricy,
France, by Col. Hal of the 394th Bomb Group, 9th Air Force. It was
probably repaired by the 584th Bomb Squadron, as it carries their unit
code, K5-T. It was later turned over to the 370th Fighter Group. Hutch-
inson, via Crow

Ma Cherie, a P-51 of the 402nd Fighter Squadron, 370th Fighter Group. *Ian MacKenzie*

My Darling Barbara IV, a P-51 piloted by 1st Lt. James J. Ward of the 402nd Fighter Squadron, 370th Fighter Group. Lt. Ward is credited with one Me 109 destroyed and 0.5 on damage to another. Both were on December 17, 1944, over Simmerath. *Ian MacKenzie*

LITTLE SANDY, a P-51 piloted by Lt. D. R. Boyett of the 402nd Fighter Squadron, 370th Fighter Group. Boyett's crew chief was Sgt. H. L. Collins and H. T. Heyen was his armorer. *Ian MacKenzie*

Draggin' Seeds, a P-51 piloted by 2nd Lt. Robert W. Blandin of the 402nd Fighter Squadron, 370th Fighter Group. Brandin is credited with damaging a Me 109 on December 17, 1944, while flying a P-38. *Ian MacKenzie*

HOT SHOT CHARLIE, a P-51 piloted by 2nd Lt. Charles E. Nelson of the 402nd Fighter Squadron, 370th Fighter Group. Nelson scored one Fw 190 confirmed and one unconfirmed on December 17, 1944, while flying a P-38. *Ian MacKenzie*

Jeanne, a P-51 piloted by Lt. Joe Breckler of the 402nd Fighter Squadron, 370th Fighter Group. His ground crew included T/Sgt. M. C. Hieser, S/Sgt. J. Smozanitz, and Sgt. R. H. Anderson. *Ian MacKenzie*

Queen of San Joaquin V, a P–51 piloted by Lt. Bert Lowe of the 402nd Fighter Squadron, 370th Fighter Group. The ground crew included T/Sgt. R. Magee, Sgt. H. Wilcoxon, Cpl. J. Nickell, and Cpl. Rogers. *Ian MacKenzie*

BUBBY HONEY, a P–51 piloted by Lt. Sam Goldman of the 402nd Fighter Squadron, 370th Fighter Group. *Ian MacKenzie*

Mickey IV, a P–51 piloted by 1st Lt. Elbert W. Lineker of the 402nd Fighter Squadron, 370th Fighter Group. Lt. Lineker destroyed one Fw 190 while flying a P–38. His ground crew included T/Sgt. H. Banta, Cpl. H. Luikhart, and Cpl. E. Encinias. *Ian MacKenzie*

Sierra Sue II, a P–51 piloted by 2nd Lt. Robert H. Bohna of the 402nd Fighter Squadron, 370th Fighter Group. Lt. Bohna is credited with downing one Fw 190. His ground crew included S/Sgt. E. Hughes, Sgt. R. Gritton, and Cpl. R. Miller. *Ian MacKenzie*

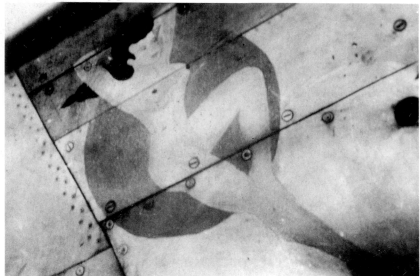

Nancy Lee, a P–51 piloted by Lt. Baggett of the 402nd Fighter Squadron, 370th Fighter Group. *Ian MacKenzie*

Mrs. Wabbit IV, a P–51 piloted by Lt. Hirsch of the 402nd Fighter Squadron, 370th Fighter Group. *Ian MacKenzie*

Pennsy Lady II, a P–38 piloted by 2nd Lt. Joseph A. Kuhn of the 401st Fighter Squadron, 370th Fighter Group, 9th Air Force. Kuhn is credited with one aerial victory. He is shown here with Crew Chief T/Sgt Pray. *P–38 National Association, via Joe Kuhn*

SASSY BABY II, a P–38 piloted by Capt. Peterson, flight leader of the 401st Fighter Squadron, 370th Fighter Group. *P–38 National Association, via Joe Kuhn*

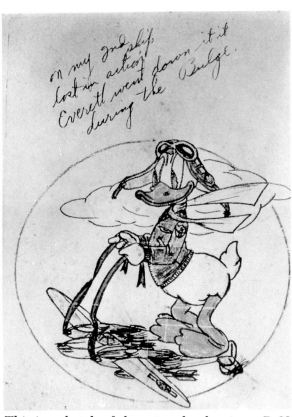

This is a sketch of the artwork adorning a P–38 piloted by Lt. Joseph A. Kuhn of the 401st Fighter Squadron, 370th Fighter Group. This was Kuhn's second plane and was lost while being flown by another pilot. *Joe Kuhn*

Vivacious Virgin II/TARGET FOR TONITE, a P–38J piloted by 1st Lt. Ian B. MacKenzie of the 402th Fighter Squadron, 370th Fighter Group. *Ian MacKenzie*

Vivacious Virgin III, a P–51 piloted by 1st Lt. Ian B. MacKenzie. Lt. MacKenzie's fuselage code was E6–T. It was in this aircraft that he is credited with damaging an Me 262. *Ian MacKenzie*

Princess Irene, "Ma Petite Cherie", a P-51 of the 402nd Fighter Squadron, 370th Fighter Group. *Ian MacKenzie*

Daisy June, a P-51 of the 402nd Fighter Squadron, 370th Fighter Group. *Ian MacKenzie*

B' Cominbac, a P-47 piloted by 1st Lt. Clarence L. Hough, 412th Fighter Squadron, 373rd Fighter Group. *B' Cominbac* was to be returned to the states after her 213th mission for a bond selling tour with her crew. After her 212th mission the new CO had the art work removed to make the plane more presentable. The effort was wasted because *B' Cominbac* was shot down on her 213th mission. *AFM*

DURK'S DOTTY!, a P-47 of the 404th Fighter Squadron, 371st Fighter Group, 9th Air Force. *Rons, via Crow*

Piccadilly Commando, a P-47 piloted by Capt. Samual Marshall of the 411th Fighter Squadron, 373rd Fighter Group. *Byers, via Crow*

Dorothy K, a P-47 piloted by Lt. Talmage Ambrose of the 410th Fighter Squadron, 373rd Fighter Group. On April 8, 1945 Lt. Ambrose shot down four long nose Fw 190s in the vicinity of Hildensheim. *B. Hess*

A P-47 of the 373rd Fighter Group. *Campbell*

A P-47 of the 373rd Fighter Group. *Miller, via Crow*

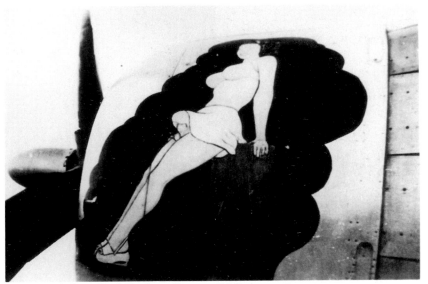

A P-47 of the 373rd Fighter Group. *Miller, via Crow*

Stardust, a P-47 of the 373rd Fighter Group. *Miller, via Crow*

Lady June, a P-47 of the 373rd Fighter Group. *Campbell*

MARY JANE, a P–47 of the 373rd Fighter Group. *Campbell*

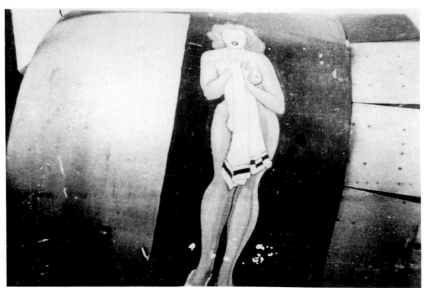

A P–47 of the 373rd Fighter Group. *Campbell*

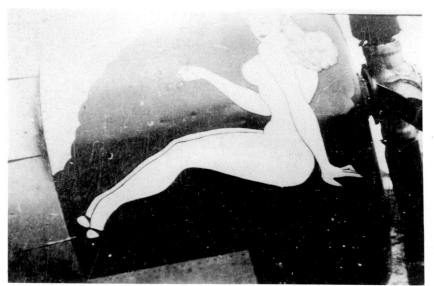

A P–47 of the 373rd Fighter Group. *Campbell*

A P–47 piloted by 1st Lt. Everett E. Peters of the 412th Fighter Squadron, 373rd Fighter Group. Peters is credited with destroying two Fw 190s and one Me 190. *Byers, via Crow*

LEMMON *Express,* a P–47 piloted by Maj. James Lemmon, CO of the 411th Fighter Squadron, 373rd Fighter Group. *Byers, via Crow*

GAL-O-MY-DREAMS, a P–47D–30–RE (code R3–A, s/n 43–3288) piloted by Lt. Staryl C. Austin, Jr., of the 410th Fighter Squadron, 373rd Fighter Group. *AFM*

A P–47 of the 373rd Fighter Group. *Campbell*

VIVIAN, a P–47 of the 507th Fighter Squadron, 404th Fighter Group, 9th Air Force. Shown are three flight leaders of the 404th who each completed their 100th mission in *VIVIAN*. Left to right are Lt. John Rogers, Jr., Lt. John Phelps and Lt. Rufus Cox, Jr. *AFM*

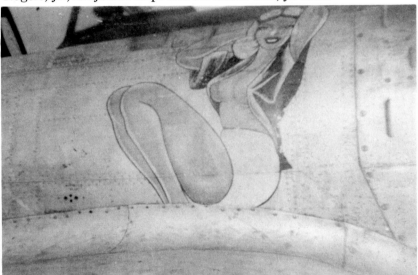

A P–47 of the 404th Fighter Group. Photo taken at St. Trond, Belgium. *Cerrone, via Crow*

CHICAGO FAT CAT, a P–47 piloted by 2nd Lt. Robert J. Reese of the 509th Fighter Squadron, 405th Fighter Group, 9th Air Force. Lt. Reese is credited with one aerial victory. The picture was taken in Belgium, 1945. *O'Neil, via Crow*

STINKEY, a P–47 piloted by Lt. Erickson of the 509th Fighter Squadron, 405th Fighter Group. Pictured left to right are Sgt. Peterson and Cpl. Murphy. Photo taken at St. Dizier, France, 1944. *O'Neil, via Crow*

LITTLE JOE III, a P-47 piloted by Joseph J. O'Neil of the 509th Fighter Squadron, 405th Fighter Group. Photo taken at Kitzingen, Germany, 1945. *O'Neil, via Crow*

JABO, a P-47 piloted by 2nd Lt. Robert Hartmann of the 509th Fighter Squadron, 405th Fighter Group. Hartmann is credited with one aerial victory. On April 11, 1945, he was killed in action. *O'Neil, via Crow*

LOOK "NO HANDS", a P-47D (code G9–E, s/n 42–27210) piloted by Maj. Chester Van Etten, of the 509th Fighter Squadron, 405th Fighter Group. Photo taken at Hasselt, Belgium, April 1945. *Nelson, via Crow*

El Texano, a P-47 piloted by Capt. Oscar Theis of the 509th Fighter Squadron, 405th Fighter Group. *Titre, via Crow*

"BALLS OUT", a P-47 piloted by Lt. M. Thompson of the 509th Fighter Squadron, 405th Fighter Group. *Titre, via Crow*

CHOW HOUND, a P-47 piloted by Lt. Blackburn of the 509th Fighter Squadron, 405th Fighter Group. Lt. Blackburn was killed in action. *Titre, via Crow*

Flak!!, NO 8, a P–47 of the 509th Fighter Squadron, 405th Fighter Group. *Titre, via Crow*

THE VIRGIN, a P–47 piloted by Lt. Leslie W. Thompson of the 509th Fighter Squadron, 405th Fighter Group. Thompson is credited with damaging an Fw 190, on March 1, 1945. *Titre, via Crow*

OFF LIMITS TO ALL TROOPS, a P–47 piloted by "Hank" Bakker of the 509th Fighter Squadron, 405th Fighter Group. *Titre, via Crow*

HONEY-BUCKET JOEL, a P–47 piloted by Lt. Doyle of the 509th Fighter Squadron, 405th Fighter Group. *Titre, via Crow*

CHIEF SKI-U-MAH, a P–47 piloted by Lt. D. E. Buholz, "Chief Of The Sioux", of the 509th Fighter Squadron, 405th Fighter Group. *Titre, via Crow*

Picture of the artwork on *CHIEF-SKI-U-MAH*. *Titre, via Crow*

RAGGEDY ANN, a P-47 of the 509th Fighter Squadron, 405th Fighter Group. Photo taken at St. Dizier, France, 1944. *O'Neil, via Crow*

A P-47 of the 509th Fighter Squadron, 405th Fighter Group. Photo taken at St. Dizier, France, 1944. *O'Neil, via Crow*

A P-47 of the 509th Fighter Squadron, 405th Fighter Group. *O'Neil, via Crow*

The Nut Cracker, putting the squeeze on Hitler, a P-47 of the 509th Fighter Squadron, 405th Fighter Group. *Titre, via Crow*

Anne, a P-47 of the 509th Fighter Squadron, 405th Fighter Group. *Titre, via Crow*

TANGO TERRY, a P-47 of the 509th Fighter Squadron, 405th Fighter Group. *Titre, via Crow*

Gladys, a P–47 of the 512th Fighter Squadron, 406th Fighter Group, 9th Air Force. *Maust, via Crow*

HUCKLEBERRY FINN, a P–38 of the 430th Fighter Squadron, 474th Fighter Group, 9th Air Force. Photo was taken in England, 1944.

A P–38J (s/n 42–67659), piloted by 1st Lt. John W. Ackley of the 430th Fighter Squadron, 474th Fighter Group. Ackley is credited with destroying two Me 109s, on December 17, 1944. He also shared a victory on a Fw 190 and damaged an Me 109, on December 18, 1944. *Ackley, via Crow*

BROOKLYN FLYER, a P–38 piloted by Lt. Alan T. Nash of the 430th Fighter Squadron, 474th Fighter Group. Note the teeth on the nose. *Ackley, via Crow*

FASCINATING BITCH, a P–38 piloted by Thomas J. Minola of the 429th Fighter Squadron, 474th Fighter Group. Photo taken at Florennes, Belgium, late 1944. The name of this plane was later changed to *Fascinating Flo. Minola, via Crow*

MISS ROCKET, a P–38 piloted by Lt. Nolby of the 429th Fighter Squadron, 474th Fighter Group. Left to right are Lts. Castel, Cinquemani, Clark, and Baillargeon. *Cinquemani, via Crow*

2nd Lt. Ernest M. Carsten of the 430th Fighter Squadron, 474th Fighter Group with his P–38. Lt. Carsten was KIA. *Ackley, via Crow*

SLEEPY TIME GAL, a P–38J–15–LO (s/n 44–23169) piloted by C. Perkins of the 434th Fighter Squadron, 479th Fighter Group, 8th Air Force. Artwork by Frederick C. Hayner. Picture taken at Wattisham, England, 1944. *P–38 National Association, via Joe Kuhn*

Whiffle Bird II, a P–38 of the 474th Fighter Group. Ruper, via Crow

MISS ROCKET 3RD, a P–38 piloted by Lt. Nolby of the 429th Fighter Squadron, 474th Fighter Group. Photo taken in Florennes, Belgium, late 1944.

HEADY HEDY, a P-38 of the 18th Fighter Group, 13th Air Force. The 18th, while equipped with P-40s, fought their first battle on December 7, 1941, during the Japanese attack on Pearl Harbor. Only two of their aircraft were able to get into the air and both were quickly shot down. The group fought with valor through the remaining years of the war, flying P-38s, P-39s, P-61 and P-70 night fighters. *Col. William Fowkes*

MISS AMBER, a P-38 piloted by 1st Lt. "Coffee" Coffman of the 12th Fighter Squadron, 18th Fighter Group. Coffman painted this nose art. *Col. William Fowkes*

"Prowler", a Mosquito XVI of the 653rd Recon Squadron, 25th Bombardment Group, attached to the 7th Reconnaissance Group. *AFM*

Lander 3715, a P–38 belonging to the 18th Fighter Group. The 18th moved to New Guinea in August 1944, where they flew escort missions to targets in the southern Philippines and Borneo. *Col. William Fowkes*

Phillie Baby II, a P–38 belonging to the 18th Fighter Group. *Col. William Fowkes*

PAPPY, a P–47D belonging to the 56th Fighter Group, 8th Air Force. The 56th entered combat with a fighter sweep in the area of St. Omer on April 13, 1943, and during the following two years they destroyed more enemy aircraft in aerial combat than any other fighter group of the Eighth. *AFM*

Little ANGEL, a P–38 flown by members of the 18th Fighter Group. *Col. William Fowkes*

HAWKEYE HATTIE-II, another of the 18th Fighter Group's P–38s. *Col. William Fowkes*

Tabitha, a P-61 Black Widow piloted by Hardin Ross, with Frank Fisher as radar observer, of the 425th Night Fighter Squadron, showing invasion stripes for D-Day operations. *AFM*

KOZY KOZA, a P-38 piloted by Lt. Sam Plotecia of the 392nd Fighter Squadron, 367th Fighter Group. In the winter of 1944, as the snow began to stand on the plane, Crew Chief Sgt. F. P. Pecora used cotton to fashion winter underwear for their favorite redhead. *Ed Haskamp*

Hell's Angel, a P-38 of the 18th Fighter Group. *Col. William Fowkes*

Another view of *Moonlight Cock-tail!*. Note the red nose cap and the name *Carol* on the engine cowl. *Ed Haskamp*

Butch II, a P–38 piloted by Capt. Horace M. Hartwig of the 392nd Fighter Squadron, 367th Fighter Group. On August 22, 1944, at 1940 hours, Capt. Hartwig shot down an Me-109 over Lyon. During the same battle the 367th is credited with downing seven Me 109s and three Fw 190s. *Ed Haskamp*

Moonlight Cock-tail!, a P–38 piloted by Lt. Clark "Doc" Livingston of the 392nd Fighter Squadron, 367th Fighter Group. *Ed Haskamp*

Viking 2, a P–38 piloted by Lt. James C. Paschall of the 392nd Fighter Squadron, 367th Fighter Group. Paschall named his plane *Viking* after the fierce fighting Scandinavian warriors of old, renowned for their fearlessness in combat. The picture was taken in Reims, November 1944. *367th Fighter Group, via Jack Curtis*

Sweet Sybil, a P–38 of the 18th Fighter Group. Note the color variations. It is quite close to today's subdued artwork on low visibility aircraft. *Col. William Fowkes*

Billy's Filly, a P–38 piloted by Col. William Fowkes of the 12th Fighter Squadron, 18th Fighter Group. This picture was taken early in 1945 in Zamboanga, Mindanao. *Col. William Fowkes*

A close-up of the nose art on *Billy's Filly.*

The unofficial 49th Fighter Squadron emblem "Fork-tailed Devils" is shown on this P–38 belonging to the 14th Fighter Group. A Luftwaffe Fighter Command pilot, on returning from a narrow escape with a P–38, referred to the P–38 as a fork-tailed devil, hence the artwork here. *S. D. Huff*

EX-LAX . . . *Shit'n'Git!* a P-51D piloted by Flight Officer Cyril B. Doleac of the 487th Fighter Squadron, 352nd Fighter Group. On August 6, 1944, Doleac shot down an Me 109 over Hamburg. *Jack Moses*

LUCKY IRISH, a P-38 piloted by Lt. Gerald O'Donnell of the 392nd Fighter Squadron, 367th Fighter Group. Lt. O'Donnell shared with Flight Officer Allen J. Diefendorf the downing of an Fw 190 over Fressancourt on August 22, 1944. *LUCKY IRISH* and O'Donnell parted company when he was forced to bail out over Eindhover. After landing he was captured and spent the remainder of the war as a prisioner. *367th Fighter Group, via Jack Curtis*

This P-51D shows the "Satans Angels" emblem of the 431st Fighter Squadron, 475th Fighter Group. The 431st flew P-51s from 1946 through 1949. *AFM*

"MISS ROGERS", a P-51D piloted by Lt. James D. Callahan of the 4th Fighter Squadron, 52nd Fighter Group. Lt. Callahan is credited with an aerial victory against an Me 109 on November 5, 1944. The group earned a DUC on June 9, 1944, for actions in Germany and August 31, 1944, for actions in Rumania. *AFM*

"*Little Buckaroo*", a P–38 piloted by R. C. "Buck" Rogers of the 392nd Fighter Squadron, 367th Fighter Group,. *367th Fighter Group via Jack Curtis*

TIKA IV, a P–51D belonging to the 374th Fighter Squadron, 361st Fighter Group. The 361st joined the 8th Air Force in England in November 1943. They served primarily as an escort organization, covering the penetration, attack, and withdrawal of bomber formations attacking targets on the continent.

"Kay-N-Tucky", a P–47 of the 318th Fighter Group, 7th Air Force. Photo dates from summer of '45, on Ie Shima. Note the high visibility diagonal black and yellow tail markings of the 318th. *Rick McGowen*

A close-up view of the nose art on *KAY-N-TUCKY*. *Rick McGowen*

Queen Mary, a P–47D of the 318th Fighter Group. *Rick McGowen*

Margie, a P–47 of the 318th Fighter Group. *Rick McGowen*

BAR FLIES, a P–47 sporting the insignia of the 73rd Fighter Squadron, 318th Fighter Group. The pilot, Lt. Robert W. Redfield, shot down a Frank on August 8, 1945, in the Shimabara Wan area. On the same day, Lt. Frederick S. Johnson shot down a Jack. These were the last two aerial victories of the 73rd Fighter Squadron, who had a combined score of twenty-two aerial victories, two probables and two damaged from November 22, 1944, to August 8, 1945. *Rick McGowen*

Dream Gal, a P–47 of the 318th Fighter Group. *Rick McGowen*

Millie, a P–47 of the 318th Fighter Group. *Rick McGowen*

BUGS III, a P-47 of the 318th Fighter Group. *Rick McGowen*

MAD RUSSIAN, a P-47 of the 318th Fighter Group. *Rick McGowen*

Sack Happy, a P-47 of the 318th Fighter Group. *Rick McGowen*

Some Punkins, a P-47 of the 318th Fighter Group. *Rick McGowen*

This ME-109 of the 79th Fighter Group in North Africa is one of several 109s which were captured and flown by our pilots. *W. Bodie*

"*Miss Kat*", a P-40 piloted by Lt. Lawrence N. Succop of the 7th Fighter Squadron, 49th Fighter Group. *E. McDowell*

Official Flying Tiger hat pin.

106

Pictured here we see members of the AVG. Seated (left to right) are Bob Smith, Ken Jernstedt, Bob Prescott, "Link" Laughlin, Bill Reed and standing are Tom Haywood (left) and Arvid Olson. *Donnie Watts*

A P–40 of the AVG belonging to 1st Lt. Robert T. Smith who was leader of the 3rd Pursuit Squadron in Kunming, China, 1942. *Donnie Watts*

A collage of insignias designed by the Walt Disney team for the war effort. Many aircraft bore Disney-inspired nose art. *Disney Display, Disney World*

Tulie, Scotty & ?, an RF–51K piloted by B. W. Scott of the 45th Tactical Recon Squadron. The wing tips, stabilizer tips and prop spinner are all blue with a white polka-dot design. The photo was taken at K-47 Chin Chan, Korea in the summer of 1952. *Jeff Ethell*

Betty Jane, an RF–51 of the 45th Tactical Recon Squadron. Note the polka-dot design on the spinner. *Jeff Ethell*

BETTY BOOTS, an F–86F piloted by Capt. Karl K. Dittmer of El Reno, Oklahoma. He was assigned to the 335th Fighter Interceptor Squadron and is credited with the destruction of three MiG fighter planes. *Donnie Watts*

WHAM BAM, an F–86F, (code FU–831, s/n 51–2831),piloted by Lt. Martin Bambrick of the 335th Fighter Interceptor Squadron, 4th Fighter Interceptor Wing. Lt. Bambrick is credited with 1 MiG on the 4th of September 1952. Note the "Bugs Bunny" artwork. The photo was taken during the summer of 1952. *Donnie Watts*

Captain Clifford D. Jolley shows off the war paint on his "skid lid". Capt. Jolley had seven confirmed aerial victories over Korea. He was assigned to the 335th Fighter Interceptor Squadron, 4th Fighter Interceptor Wing. *Donnie Watts*

NEWARK FIRE BALL, an F–86E (s/n 51–2794) of the 335th Fighter Interceptor Squadron, 4th Fighter Interceptor Wing at Kimpo in 1953.

GOPHER PATROL, an F–86E–10, from the 335th Fighter Interceptor Squadron, 4th Fighter Interceptor Group, Kempo. The 335th Fighter Interceptor Squadron had more aerial victories than any other Fighter Interceptor Squadron in Korea. *Donnie Watts*

BOB-BEEP-VAL, an F–86F of the 335th Fighter Interception Squadron. This is believed to be the aircraft of Capt. Robert J. Love. Capt. Love is credited with six MiGs destroyed. *Campbell*

BLACK DAN, an F–86F of the 336th Fighter Interceptor Squadron. *Donnie Watts*

The pilot in this shot is doing his ground inspection pre-flight prior to a mission up North. This F–86F shows the yellow markings of the 336th Fighter Interceptor Squadron. *Campbell*

Hot F–86Fs of the 334th Fighter Interceptor Squadron are parked at the ready. The F–86 with s/n 51-0625 shows fourteen aerial victories. *Donnie Watts*

At 30,000 feet plus we have a rare and beautiful view of two "hunters" on the prowl, with 80% cloud cover below and drop tanks still attached. These two will continue to search for MiGs crossing the 38th parallel. *Campbell*

O'L ANCHOR ASS, an F–51 of the 36th Fighter Interceptor Squadron shows the "Flying Fiend" emblem, which has been the official emblem for the 36th Squadron since its approval on June 13, 1931. *Jeff Ethell*

MAC'S REVENGE was the name on the port side of *O'L ANCHOR ASS*, which was piloted by Maj. William O'Donnell, CO of the 36th Fighter Interceptor Squadron. Although the F–51 which had been so successful in WWII had been put in storage and replaced by the newer F–80C, the 8th Fighter Group, who had transitioned into the Shooting Star during the latter part of 1949 and had not become proficient in its use, were re-equipped with the more familiar F–51. *Jeff Ethell*

111

Two F–86F Sabre Jets headed up North of the Yalu river in search of MiGs, Yaks and other targets of opportunity.

NINA, an F–86 (code FU–832) piloted by Col. John Mitchell of the 39th Fighter Interceptor Squadron. Col. Mitchell is credited with four MiG – 15s, the first on January 21, 1953, and the fourth on May 5, 1953. All four victories were in F–86s. *Jeff Ethell*

An F–51 on a typical dirt airstrip in South Korea. Note the small makeshift hangers. *Campbell*

PANTHER QUEEN, an F–80C of the 35th Fighter Bomber Squadron, 8th Bomber Wing, Itazuke Air Base, in Japan. Photo taken in 1954. *via Donnie Watts*

SCAT VI, a P-51 piloted by Maj. Robin Olds of the 434th Fighter Squadron, 479th Fighter Group. Maj. Olds is credited with thirteen aerial victories in WWII and another four in Vietnam. *via Hess/Ivie*

GIVE M HELL FOR HL, a P-38 of the 434th Fighter Squadron, 479th Fighter Group piloted by Capt. Claire A. P. Duffie. Capt. Duffie had three confirmed aerial victories—all Me 109s. *B. Hess*

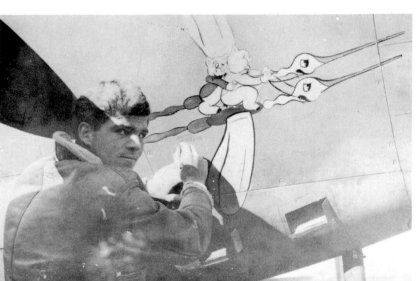

Locked-Wing Dragon Flies, the 329th Fighter Group insignia. Picture shows Frederick C. Hayner with a P-38 of the 329th Fighter Group, January 1, 1944, at Orange County Airport. Hayner was first rate artist. *P-38 National Association, via Joe Kuhn*

SPARKY JUNIOR 2ND, a P-38, pilot and group unknown. This veteran P-38 boasts of five enemy aircraft destroyed, along with numerous fighter sweeps, umbrella cover, and bombing missions. *Crow*

SPARE PARTS, a P-51B dropped into the sea while being unloaded at Liverpool. It was recovered and sent to Warton to be dismantled for spare parts. The mechanics there rebuilt it as a two-seater in their spare time. *via Jeff Ethell*

JUGHEAD "LET GO ME EARS", a P-38 that was at the Army Air Depot in Warton, England for repairs. *Art Lobolzke*

Flying Skullmen, a P–40 showing an insignia that was common on planes of the 85th Fighter Squadron, 79th Fighter Group, 9th Air Force. Pictured left to right are Lt. Robert J. Duffield, Lt. Raymond Higgins, and Lt. Martin J. Grandbery. *OASM*

Mediterranean Theater

Even without an enemy to fight, the living conditions in North Africa would have been miserable. Pilots and ground crews alike slept on the ground in tents during freezing nights, refueled, armed and maintained aircaft in the blazing heat, ate poor food and tried to keep the ever-present blowing sand out of everything. The highlight of a day was often a few eggs traded from the local Berber tribesmen.

The streets of local towns were full of dirty children begging for cigarettes, gum and chocolate. When sleeping on the ground became unbearable, a fox hole was dug, a pup tent stretched over the top, a sleeping bag stuffed in and home, sweet home hung on the outside. In the great flat lands of the desert, where an outhouse would have been a much appreciated luxury, crews weren't even afforded the privacy of a nearby tree. Water, continually in short supply, was available for drinking or brushing teeth only—except when it rained. Then there was plenty of water with the impressive byproduct of boot sucking, airplane swallowing mud.

The Army Air Forces in the Mediterranean Theater of Operations (MTO) lived a nomadic existence, starting with the 9th Air Force in June 1942. After the arrival of B–24s and B–17s in Egypt, the 57th Fighter Group arrived in Palestine after flying its P–40s off the aircraft carrier USS *Ranger*. Without any realistic combat training in the United States, the group's pilots were assigned ground support for the British 8th Army which was being hard pressed by Gen. Erwin Rommel's Afrika Korps. More P–40s arrived with the 79th Fighter Group in November and the 324th Fighter Group in December. Though their Curtiss fighters were supposedly inferior to German Bf 109s, the men flying them gave as good as they got.

On 8 November 1942 Operation Torch, the Allied invasion of North Africa, began under the support of the 12th Air Force, which had been formed out of the 8th Air Force in England to take control of several bomb groups as well as the 1st, 14th and 82nd Fighter Groups (P–38s), 31st and 52nd Fighter Groups (Spitfires), 81st Fighter Group (P–39s), 3rd Photo Group (F–4s, F–5s) and the 350th Fighter Group (P–39s). By the end of the year American fighter pilots were up against the Luftwaffe's

This was not an unusual sight in North Africa, the members of the 79th Fighter Group sitting around the tent during meal time. The shape of the tent is due to the strong winds and the deep tracks in the softer dirt mark where the men bogged down in the mud after the heavy rains. *Frank and Freida Sanders*

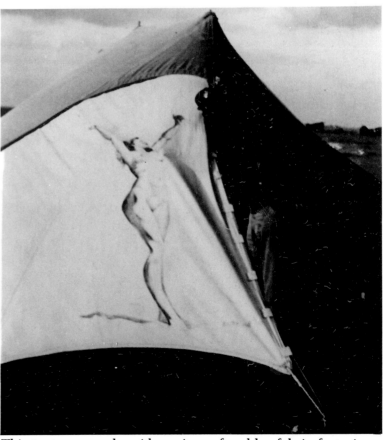

This tent was made with a piece of rudder fabric featuring a femme fatale from a downed P-40. *Frank and Freida Sanders*

best, taking terrible losses while learning the lessons of combat the hard way. It was here that the P–38 proved to be an outstanding all-round fighter, able to perform bomber escort as well as effective ground support. Soon there were several Warhawk and Lightning aces.

By May 1943, when the Germans surrendered in Tunisia, fighter strength in the MTO was increasing due to the addition of such units as the all-black 99th Fighter Squadron, which later joined the all-black 332nd Fighter Group. Sicily was pounded into surrender as Montgomery's 8th and Patton's 7th Armies moved through, then Italy was invaded. When the 9th Air Force moved up to the ETO late in the year, several groups were transferred to the 12th and the strategic 15th Air Force was formed to bomb Germany from bases in Italy, which had surrendered in September. By early 1944, while the 12th continued to hit tactical targets with P–47s and medium bombers, the 15th was on its way up to Germany supported by P–38s and P–51s.

From March through May 1944 the 12th's P–47s, A–20s, B–25s and B–26s were heavily committed to Operation Strangle, the interdiction of enemy lines of communication across the narrow waist of Italy while the 15th's fighters were slugging it out with the Luftwaffe

from Rome to Ploesti to Austria. From the deck to 35,000 feet Allied air power had slowly encircled the Germans from all sides by the end of the year. When the surrender came in May 1945 American fighters roamed the skies at will.

Due to the 12th's primary ground support mission, it produced but fifty-nine aces—with the 82nd Group's William "Dixie" Sloan coming out on top with twelve victories while flying P–38s, followed by Levi Chase (ten) of the 33rd and Frank Hurlbut (nine) of the 82nd. When the 15th AF was created, much of the fighter versus fighter air war went with it along with many up-and-coming 12th AF aces. Though in combat for only a year and a half, the 15th ended up with ninety-three aces. The 31st Fighter Group's John J. Voll was at the top of the list with twenty-one kills, followed by Herschel Green (eighteen) of the 325th Group, James Varnell (seventeen) of the 52nd and Sam Brown (fifteen) of the 31st.

The Mediterranean turned out to be anything but the soft underbelly Winston Churchill had promised. From the blowing sand of North Africa to the frigid skies of Germany, fighter pilots did what was asked of them, often at great cost but never without ever-increasing skill and determination.

The markings on this P–38 of the 27th Fighter Squadron, 1st Fighter Group indicate a very active and successful career. *OASM*

"Shoot . . . You're Faded," a P–38 piloted by 2nd Lt. John A. Mackay of the 27th Fighter Squadron, 1st Fighter Group. Lt. Mackay is credited with five aerial victories. Note the skull and crossbones on the tip of the nose. *OASM*

OLD RUSTY, a P–38 of the 94th Fighter Squadron, 1st Fighter Group, piloted by Warren "Beans" Campbell while stationed in Salsola, Foggia, Italy, summer 1944. *Jack Ilfrey*

OLD MAN MOE, a P–38 of the 1st Fighter Group. This ghost appears to take great pleasure in kicking the bucket bearing the image of Hitler. *Mrs. D. Starbuck, via Jack Ilfrey*

Jolly Roger, a P–38 of the 1st Fighter Group with the well known pirate flag bearing the skull and crossbones. *Mrs. D. Starbuck, via Jack Ilfrey*

HELLZAPOPPIN, a P–38 of the 1st Fighter Group showing Donald Duck aiming a cannon. *Mrs. D. Starbuck, via Jack Ilfrey*

AUNT MINNIE'S BOWSER, a P–38 of the 27th Fighter Squadron, 1st Fighter Group. Anything but a lap dog, Bowser looks quite intimidating. *Mrs. D. Starbuck, via Jack Ilfrey*

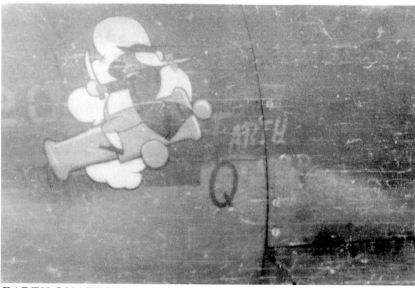

EARTH QUAKER, a P–38 of the 1st Fighter Group with a Quaker riding a cannon and wielding a sword. *Mrs. D. Starbuck, via Jack Ilfrey*

A P–38 assigned to the 94th Fighter Squadron, 1st Fighter Group. The artist is applying the finishing touches to a frightened Hitler with his fingers plugging his ears. *Jack Ilfrey*

DING HOW, a P–38 of the 1st Fighter Group. Standing by the painting of a circus clown is Armorer John Machinovitch of the 94th Fighter Squadron, 1st Fighter Group. *Jack Ilfrey*

LIBERTY BELLE, a P–38 (code 44–25782) piloted by Lt. Harry Eberhardt of the 94th Fighter Squadron, 1st Fighter Group. Inside a bell-shaped background is a painting of a Varga girl. Pictured with the P–38 is Armorer John Machinovitch. *H. Eberhardt, via Jack Ilfrey*

A P–38 of the 1st Fighter Group with a caricature of a fighter pilot wearing head gear and goggles. He is sitting on a magic carpet and dreaming of far away places. *Mrs. D. Starbuck, via Jack Ilfrey*

"MIGHTY MITE," a P–38 assigned to the 94th Fighter Squadron, 1st Fighter Group. This little guy in armor is ready for the joust. *Jack Ilfrey*

TEXAS TERROR, boom art on a P–38F-LO (code UN-O, s/n 41–7587) piloted by Capt. Jack Ilfrey, 94th Fighter Squadron, 1st Fighter Group. Ilfrey became the first P–38 ace, on December 26, 1942. *Jack Ilfrey*

HAPPY JACK'S GO BUGGY, a P–38 piloted by Capt. Jack Ilfrey while in the 94th Fighter Squadron, 1st Fighter Group. *Jack Ilfrey*

1st Lt. Richard J. Lee, a P–38 pilot of the 94th Fighter Squadron, 1st Fighter Group, wearing the DFC he earned on his first mission. Lee scored five aerial victories. *Jeff Ethell*

SWEET SUE, a P–38 assigned to the 94th Fighter Squadron, 1st Fighter Group. *Jack Ilfrey*

THE OLD SOLDIER NEVER DIES, a P–38 of the 94th Fighter Squadron, 1st Fighter Group. *Jack Ilfrey*

FLYING RANGER, a P–38 of the 1st Fighter Group. This Ranger is Texan from the top of his ten-gallon hat to the bottom of wooly-chaps. *Mrs. D. Starbuck, via Jack Ilfrey*

Mon Amy, a P–38 piloted by Herbert B. Hatch, Jr., of the 71st Fighter Squadron, 1st Fighter Group. Hatch became an ace on June 10, 1944, destroying five Fw 190s. *AFM*

"DEAR JOHN", another veteran P–38, believed to belong to the 79th Fighter Squadron, 1st Fighter Group. *Jeff Ethell*

The ground crew of this P–38 parked at an airfield in Italy are members of the 94th Fighter Squadron, 1st Fighter Group. Note the spiraling on the spinners, the eight-balls on the engine cowl and the checkerboard pattern on the nose. *Jeff Ethell*

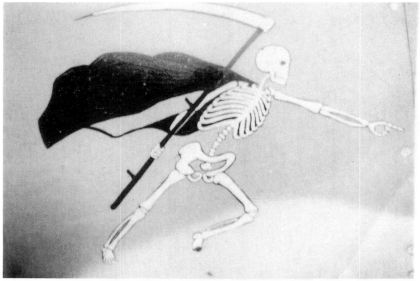

This unidentified P–38 has its version of the Grim Reaper as a caped skeleton struggling forward against a strong wind. *Jack Ilfrey*

"*Mocambo Commando II*", a P–38 piloted by Maj. Kenneth A. Gaskin, CO of the 37th Fighter Squadron, 14th Fighter Group. Maj. Gaskin is credited with three aerial victories, all on April 4, 1944. *S. D. Huff*

Pat III, a P–38 flown by Col. Oliver B. Taylor, CO of the 14th Fighter Group. Taylor scored five confirmed aerial victories. *S. D. Huff*

"FIGHTING IRISHMAN", a P–38 (s/n 42–104135) piloted by Lt. O'Toole of the 49th Fighter Squadron, 14th Fighter Group. O'Toole is pictured with S/Sgt. Hunter, Cpl. Merack, and Cpl. May. *MAFB*

BAD PENNY, a P–38 piloted by 1st Lt. Lloyd K. DeMoss of the 49th Fighter Squadron, 14th Fighter Group. DeMoss scored four victories and was a member of the first fighter group to see action in the African invasion. S. D. Huff

"EARTHQUAKE McGOON", a P–38 piloted by 1st Lt. Richard A. Campbell of the 37th Fighter Squadron, 14th Fighter Group. Lt. Campbell was awarded the Air Medal and seven OLC and is credited with six enemy aircraft destroyed, one probable, and two damaged. S. D. Huff

JEWBOY, a P–38, piloted by 2nd Lt. Philip M. Goldstein of the 49th Fighter Squadron, 14th Fighter Group. JEWBOY also appeared on the starboard side of the aircraft, only on that side it was written in German. Goldstein destroyed three and damaged two enemy aircraft. S. D. Huff

Gerry, a P–38, piloted by Maj. Nathan M. Abbott of the 49th Fighter Squadron. He scored four aerial victories. Left to right are Victor Mosseau, Abbott, T/Sgt. Summerlin, and Doc Hunter. On the cowling is the "The Forked-Tailed Devils" insignia. S. D. Huff

Princess, a P–38, piloted by Lt. Enoch P. Lemon of the 37th Fighter Squadron, 14th Fighter Group. When Lemon was assigned this P–38 and asked what name he wanted on it, he said, "Princess" (his pet name for his wife, Dorsey). He is credited with three aerial victories. S. D. Huff

MISS N PARTZ, a P–38 of the 14th Fighter Group, pictured with Crew Chiefs Hubb Bennett and Tom Mackey. S. D. Huff

SORTA PISTOF, a P–38 piloted by Flight Officer Jack Hohman of the 48th Fighter Squadron, 14th Fighter Group. Hohman is credited with four aerial victories. *S. D. Huff*

STONEWALL HONEY, a P–38 piloted by 2nd Lt. William A. Blocker of the 48th Fighter Squadron, 14th Fighter Group. Blocker is credited with a probable Me 109, on May 6, 1944. *S. D. Huff*

Joyce, a P–38 piloted by Lt. Cleveland J. Tatum of the 37th Fighter Squadron, 14th Fighter Group. Lt. Tatum scored three aerial victories. *S. D. Huff*

"PISTOL PACKING MAMA"/Murph, a P–38 (s/n 42–104275) piloted by 2nd Lt. William O. White of the 37th Fighter Squadron, 14th Fighter Group. White destroyed one Me 110. *S. D. Huff*

Beverly, a P–38 piloted by Maj. Henry H. Trollope of the 49th Fighter Squadron, 14th Fighter Group. Trollope, 49th Squadron CO, is pictured here with Lt. Col. Troy Keith, group CO. *S. D. Huff*

SWEET LORRAINE II, a P–38 piloted by 1st Lt. Harold Simmons of the 49th Fighter Squadron, 14th Fighter Group. Simmons destroyed an Fw 190 and damaged another. *S. D. Huff*

IRENE 5TH, a P–38 piloted by Capt. William R. Palmer of the 49th Fighter Squadron, 14th Fighter Group. Capt. Palmer destroyed an Me 210 and an Me 109 and damaged two more. *S. D. Huff*

Shugar II, a P–38 piloted by 2nd Lt. Herbert C. Schoener of the 49th Fighter Squadron, 14th Fighter Group. Schoener scored one aerial victory. *S. D. Huff*

Murl Girl, a P–38 piloted by 1st Lt. Wesley C. Hancock of the 37th Fighter Squadron, 14th Fighter Group. Lt. Hancock destroyed one Me 109. *S. D. Huff*

"*KNIPTION*", a P–38 piloted by Lt. Virgil H. Smith of the 48th Fighter Squadron, 14th Fighter Group. Smith is credited with six aerial victories. *Jack Ilfrey*

BARBARA, a P–38 piloted by Lt. Oliver Bryant of the 49th Fighter Squadron, 14th Fighter Group. Bryant shot down an Me 109 on December 6, 1944. *S. D. Huff*

PRINCESS RITA, a P-38, probably from the 49th Fighter Squadron. This aircraft served in Italy, North Africa, and Tunisia with the 14th Fighter Group. In the picture is Tom Mickey, the armorer. *S. D. Huff*

Geronimo!, a P-40N of the 45th Squadron, 15th Fighter Group on Nanumes Island. Note that while the aircraft is being armed a tarp is placed over the cockpit to keep it cooler inside. *E. McDowell*

Manaleene, an A-36 piloted by Mark A. "Doc" Savage of the 522nd Fighter Squadron, 27th Fighter Group. Photo taken on the Salerno beachhead, Italy, 1943. *AFM*

VICTORY, P-51 tail art proclaims the news. Colonel Marion Malcolm, CO, and Lt. Col. Woodrow B. Wilmot, deputy CO, pictured with the pilots and crew chiefs of the 5th Fighter Squadron, 52nd Fighter Group on V-E Day, 1945. *MAFB*

Doris-Faye II, another P-51 piloted by Lt. Col. Charles W. Boedeker, deputy CO of the 52nd Fighter Group. This P-51D replaced the P-51B Boedeker had originally named *Doris-Faye*. Pictured with Lt. Boedeker is S/Sgt. Edwin M. Brown, his crew chief. *MAFB*

Lady Jane II, a P-51 Mustang piloted by 1st Lt. Stanley Pell of the 4th Fighter Squadron, 52nd Fighter Group. *MAFB*

Doris-Faye, a P–51 piloted by Lt. Col. Charles W. Boedeker of the 5th Fighter Squadron, 52nd Fighter Group. Boedeker scored two aerial victories. *MAFB*

A P–51 piloted by Capt. James Varnell of the 2nd Fighter Squadron, 52nd Fighter Group. Varnell is credited with 17 aerial victories. Seated in the cockpit is S/Sgt. Elmer Dalebroux. Standing is Sgt. Charles Jones. Seated on the wing is Sgt. Murrell Fleming. *MAFB*

DOTTIE, a P–51 piloted by Capt. John S. Clarke, Jr., of the 2nd Fighter Squadron, 52nd Fighter Group. Capt. Clarke has 2.5 aerial victories. *DOTTIE* is pictured with members of the USO Unit Number 307 that performed for the 57th Fighter Group, on November 19, 1944. *MAFB*

Little Joe, a P–51 piloted by 2nd Lt. Joe H. Blackburn of the 5th Fighter Squadron, 52nd Fighter Group. Pictured with Crew Chief Sgt. George Hahn, Jr. *MAFB*

Scotty III, a P–51 piloted by 1st Lt. Bruno W. Dangelmaier of the 2nd Squadron, 52nd Fighter Group. Photo taken on October 6, 1944, in Madna, Italy. *MAFB*

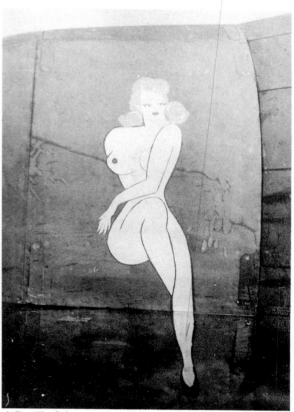

THE BAR-FLY, a P–51 piloted by 2nd Lt. Robert G. Anderson of the 52nd Fighter Group. Anderson scored one aerial victory. *MAFB*

AMERICAN BEAGLE SQUADRON, a Spitfire of the 2nd Fighter Squadron, 52nd Fighter Group. *B. Hess*

A P–47 of the 65th Fighter Squadron, 57th Fighter Group. *Hudlow, via Crow*

SPAREPARTS, a P–51 pictured with Col. Marion Malcolm, CO of the 52nd Fighter Group, and Col. Felix L. Vidal, deputy CO of the 306th Wing, posing with S/Sgt. Lawrence J. Anderson of the 5th Squadron. *MAFB*

MONK, a Spitfire piloted by Lt. Roland Wooten of the 307th Fighter Squadron, 57th Fighter Group, 12th Air Force. Wooten is shown with their mascot "flying Sgt. Monk Hunter", name-sake of Maj. Gen. Monk O. Hunter. Lt. Wooten scored three aerial victories. *MAFB*

A P–40 of the 57th Fighter Group, wearing the scorpion emblem of the 64th Fighter Squadron. Also note the star on the hubcap. *AFM*

"PONNIE", a P–47 of the 64th Fighter Squadron, 57th Fighter Group. Hidden by the wing is the emblem of the 64th Fighter Squadron: the scorpion and pyramid. *AFM*

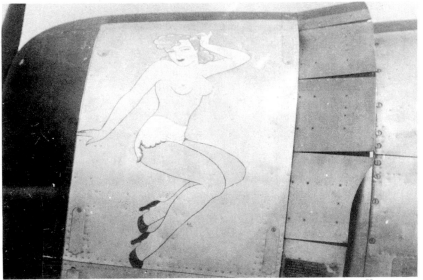

A P–47 of the 65th Fighter Squadron, 57th Fighter Group. *Hudlow, via Crow*

MUGGINS, a P–47 of the 65th Fighter Squadron, 57th Fighter Group. *Hudlow, via Crow*

A P–47 (s/n 42–26448) piloted by Lt. Lyle Duba of the 65th Fighter Squadron, 57th Fighter Group, pictured in Corsica, 1944. *Hudlow, via Crow*

A closeup view of the bird emblem on the cowl of Lt. Duba's P–47. *Hudlow, via Crow*

Sandra, a P–47 (s/n 42–27179) of the 64th Fighter Squadron, 57th Fighter Group. This P–47 also sports the 64th's scorpion emblem. *Easley, via Crow*

A P–47 of the 65th Fighter Squadron, 57th Fighter Group. Photo taken in Grossetto, Italy. *Hudlow, via Crow*

Unca Bud, a P–40F Warhawk of the 65th Fighter Squadron, 57th Fighter Group. Notice the very early national insignia. The fin flashes were added for recognition after their arrival. The aircraft was the color of desert sand. Picture taken in 1943. *AFM*

"The Tennessean", a P–40 piloted by Capt. White of the 85th Fighter Squadron, 79th Fighter Group. Pictured left to right are the members of the group known as the "The Tennessee Boys": Lt. Ryburn, Lt. Cox, Lt. Pace, and Capt. White. *MAFB*

"The Crump Machine", a P–40 piloted by Lt. Thomas E. Cox of the 85th Fighter Squadron, 79th Fighter Group. Lt. Cox is pictured here with his crew, in April of 1942. He received the DFC and Air Medal with five OLC. *MAFB*

10 GRAND, Republic's 10,000th Thunderbolt was flown on the 79th's 30,000th combat sortie by 2nd Lt. John F. Martin of the 85th Fighter Squadron in January 1945. *AFM*

Li'l Joe II, a P-40 piloted by Col. Earl E. Bates, CO of the 79th Fighter Group. *Li'l Joe II*, the only aircraft of the group bearing the group insignia, was named for his son. Col. Bates earned the DFC, Air Medal with five OLC and the British DFC. *Frank and Freida Sanders*

HELL'S BELLES, a P-40 with members of the 79th Fighter Group. *MAFB*

This P-40 of the 86th Fighter Squadron, 79th Fighter Group, bears the insignia of "The Commander". This same insignia was later carried over to their P-47's. *E. McDowell*

Irmgard, an Me-109 that was shot down by ground fire and then rebuilt to flyable condition. Note the "Skeeter" insignia of the 87th Fighter Squadron, 79th Fighter Group. Also added to the aircraft was the code X8-7. *Olmstead*

This P-47 of the 86th Fighter Squadron, 79th Fighter Group was damaged when an RAAF P-51 crashed on take-off, exploding the bomb it was carrying, killing its pilot and a 86th Fighter Squadron crew chief. Photo taken at Fano, Italy, on Dec. 17, 1944. *Short, via Crow*

P-47 of the 86th Fighter Squadron, 79th Fighter Group, at Cesenatico Air Base about to head for Yugoslavia. The insignia of the 86th Fighter Squadron "The Comanches" is on the cowling. *Short, via Crow*

The Stump Jumper, a P-40 piloted by Maj. Fred Schoellkopf of the 85th Fighter Squadron, 79th Fighter Group. Schoellkopf earned the DFC and the Air Medal with six OLC. *Frank and Freida Sanders*

Cpl. Joe Pumphrey, 79th Fighter Group artist, painting a skirt on a piece of rudder art because the general ordered that all "painted ladies" must be at least partially clothed. *Frank and Freida Sanders*

Lt. Col. John Martin, CO of the 85th Fighter Squadron admiring the artwork of Joe Pumphrey—who painted these pin-ups on the rudders of most of the squadrons' aircraft. *Hoffman, via E. McDowell*

A P-40 piloted by 1st Lt. Charles K. Bolack of the 85th Fighter Squadron, 79th Fighter Group. Bolack scored one aerial victory. *Hoffman, via E. McDowell*

Maj. Joseph W. Connelly of the 85th Fighter Squadron, 79th Fighter Group standing by the rudder art on his P-40. Connelly earned the DFC and the Air Medal with six OLC. *Frank and Freida Sanders*

Miss Memphis, rudder art on the P-40 piloted by Lt. Thomas E. Cox of the 85th Fighter Squadron, 79th Fighter Group. *Frank and Freida Sanders*

A P-47 of the 79th Fighter Group. *Short, via Crow*

KLONDIKE KLIPPER II, a P-47 of the 87th Fighter Squadron, 79th Fighter Group. Note the "Skeeter" emblem on the cowl and the lightning bolt pattern on the tail. Above we see the members of the 86th Squadron returning from a mission while the 87th is starting their engines. *Short, via Cross*

Lt. Joseph S. Michalowski of the 340th Bomb Group made many flights in this captured and repaired Me 109. Photo taken August 20, 1943, at Comiso airdrome, Sicily. It isn't known if the artwork was German or added after its capture, although it appears to be very American. *MAFB*

Skipper's Darlin' a P-51 piloted by Capt. Andrew Turner, CO of the 100th Fighter Squadron, 332nd Fighter Group. The 332nd served in Italy with the 12th Air Force. Shaking hands are Capt. Turner and Lt. Clarence P. Lester. *AFM*

Sug's Dopey, a P-51 piloted by 1st Lt. Richard W. Hall of the 100th Fighter Squadron, 332nd Fighter Group. Hall destroyed one Me 109. *AFM*

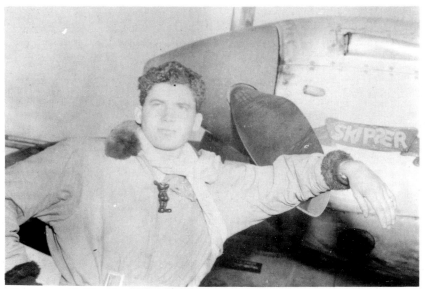

Skipper, a P–38 piloted by 1st Lt. Kenneth R. Frost of the 82nd Fighter Group. Lt. Frost is credited with destroying one twin-engine aircraft and four locomotives in strafing attacks. He was also awarded the Air Medal with OLC. *MAFB*

"SAD SACK", a P–38 piloted by Capt. Ernest K. Osher of the 95th Fighter Squadron, 82nd Fighter Group. Capt. Osher is credited with five aerial victories. Pictured with him are T/Sgt. L. G. Lee, Sgt. W. R. Coy, and Cpl. S. J. Verlarde. *Jeff Ethell*

Aerial side view of *Big "STUD"* with Lt. Col. Basler at the controls. Note the changes in artwork and lettering and the checkered tail. *MAFB*

A P–40 of No. 450 Squadron, Royal Australian Air Force. Photo taken in Italy. *Jeff Ethell*

Big "STUD", a P–47 piloted by Lt. Col. Robert Basler of the 319th Fighter Squadron, 325th Fighter Group. Basler scored six aerial victories. After his return to the states, he took his aircraft to airshows to promote the Air Force. *MAFB*

FiFi, a P-40 of the No. 450 Squadron, Royal Australian Air Force. The Australians were not as staid as the British as this shot of *FiFi* attests to. *E. McDowell*

"EL CID" LOVES JOYCE, a P-40 piloted by Lt. Sidney "El Cid" Brooks of the 332nd Fighter Group. Lt. Brooks was killed in action over Sicily. *OASM*

MISS PELT, a P-51 piloted by 2nd Lt. Clarence D. Lester of the 100th Fighter Squadron, 332nd Fighter Group. Capt. Turner is congratulating Lt. Lester after he shot down three Me 109s on July 18, 1944, over North Italy. *AFM*

KITTEN, a P-51 piloted by Capt. Charles E. McGee of the 302nd Fighter Squadron, 332nd Fighter Group. Capt. McGee is credited with one Fw 190, on August 24, 1944. Also shown here is Crew Chief S/Sgt. Nathan B. Wilson. *AFM*

Goodwiggle, a P-51 piloted by 2nd Lt. Christopher W. Newman of the 100th Fighter Squadron, 332nd Fighter Group. *AFM*

"Ina The Macon Belle," a P-51 piloted by 2nd Lt. Lee A. Archer of the 302nd Fighter Squadron, 332nd Fighter Group. Lt. Archer destroyed one Me 109 on July 18 and three more on October 12, 1944. With him is Crew Chief S/Sgt. William L. Carter. *AFM*

A Kawanishi H6K Flying boat going down in flames on May 8, 1942. This plane was shot down just prior to the Battle of Midway by Lt. Commander Charles Fenton. Although the plane was seen to crash into the water, it was credited as a probable.

Pacific Theater

American defeat and withdrawal describe the first six months of the Pacific War. Just hours after the Japanese attacked Pearl Harbor on 7 December 1941 they were hitting the Philippines, which fell in May 1942. By February they had Java, then forces landed in New Guinea and the Solomons in preparation for an invasion of Australia.

The first hints of a Japanese reversal came in early May when attempts to take Port Moresby were thwarted and the Battle of the Coral Sea was fought to a draw. The only effective American fighters to hold the fort during those dark days were the Army P-40 and the Navy Grumman F4F Wildcat. Though both were technically inferior to the Mitsubishi A6M Zero, American pilots exploited their strong points of ruggedness, high diving speed and heavy fire power to keep the top notch Imperial Japanese Navy pilots at bay.

The first American aerial victories in the Pacific were made over Pearl Harbor by surprised USAAF 46th and 47th Pursuit Squadron pilots who managed to scramble into the air, some still in their pajamas, flying P-36s and P-40s. Ten victories were claimed, four by George Welch, two by Ken Taylor and one each by four other pilots. Welch would go on to score a total of sixteen victories.

As the Japanese advanced up the Philippines they were opposed by five Army squadrons flying P-35s and P-40s. During early December, 17th Pursuit Squadron commander Boyd "Buzz" Wagner (eight victories total) made ace. When Bataan fell, there was but a single P-40 operational, patched together from parts off destroyed aircraft. Two pilots, Grant Mahoney and Andy Reynolds, made ace holding off the inevitable in Java. Those pilots who managed to escape from the Philippines and Java brought the rich lessons of combat experience into the 5th, 7th and 13th Air Forces which would be responsible for the AAF's effort in the Pacific.

US Navy fighter pilots fought against long odds to protect their carriers, escort dive and torpedo bombers, engage enemy aircraft at long distances and use their aircraft as fighter bombers while pushing all the way to Japan. Unfortunately, nose art was rare on these aircraft because Navy regulations specifically prohibited any form of individual art. From the first directives on markings and camouflage written long before World War II, it was clearly stated that no other markings of any type would be applied—this meant none! Though the rules were broken under the stress of the combat environment, it was rare.

In February 1942, the 8th, 35th and 49th Pursuit Groups arrived in Australia with P-39s and P-40s. Though Japanese bombing raids against Darwin were countered, it was not until late summer, when all three groups were flying from Port Moresby, New Guinea, that Army fighter pilots started to seriously challenge their Japanese Navy and Army counterparts. In September the 5th Air Force was formed and a new fighter, the P-38, began to arrive for the 39th Fighter Squadron. In late December 1942, the Lightning was in action for the first time with victories being claimed by several future aces. Among them was Richard Bong who would later become the American ace of aces with forty kills.

To put the war on the offensive, the 5th's bombers and fighters flew over the Owen Stanley Mountains in rotten weather. With the opening of Dobodura on the other side from Moresby, the 5th had a base from which it could hound the enemy constantly, the primary target being Lae. Wewak, further up the New Guinea coast, and Rabaul, New Britain, were being hit by mid 1943, and the P-38 quickly proved to be the ideal fighter for the theater, with long range, twin engine safety and heavy firepower. In May the Lightning equipped 475th Fighter Group was formed and in June the 348th Group arrived in the theater with P-47s, followed by another Thunderbolt outfit, the 58th, later in the year. Aces quickly emerged from the roving bands of fighters which were making a habit of never leaving the Japanese alone. As 5th AF commander George C. Kenney put it, "this means air control so supreme that the birds have to wear our air force insignia."

With Fiji and New Caledonia threatened by the massive enemy thrust after Pearl Harbor, from January through May 1942 the remnants of three AAF fighter squadrons were combined to form the 17th Pursuit Squadron with P-39s and moved to those islands. Since their aircraft lacked the range to seek the enemy out, there was very little combat, yet commanders such as John W. Mitchell constantly made pilots engage in mock dogfights to hone their skills. That was to pay off richly when the units were transferred in August 1942 to Guadalcanal to support the American invasion.

Flying from Henderson Field, the pilots soon found out the Airacobra was no match for enemy fighters. Fighting a desperate battle in the air flying both P-39s and P-40s, it was not unusual to have enemy troops come right up to the edge of the field—they often landed in the midst of infantry fire, not to mention shellings of the strip by Japanese ships. By late 1942 the three squadrons were formed into the 347th Fighter Group and served along with the newly arrived 339th Squadron with its valuable P-38s. In January 1943 the 13th Air Force was formed out

Japanese Zeke being attacked by Navy plane during action in the Pacific. Photo was taken by gun camera installed in the leading edge of the aircraft's wing. *National Archives via Kevin Grantham*

of other Pacific AAF units to provide air strength for the Solomons and the Central Pacific.

Soon the 18th Fighter Group was formed, giving the 13th AF the fighter strength it would have throughout the war. Flying in close cooperation with Marine fighter units, the 13th had an excellent balance—P–39s for ground attack, P–40s for medium altitude defense and P–38s for long range strikes into enemy territory. On 18 April 1943 one of the most famous fighter missions of the war was led by John W. Mitchell (who would end the war with eleven victories). Mitchell led sixteen P–38s over a circuitous, 700 mile route at wave top level to intercept and shoot down the two Betty bombers carrying Admiral Isoroku Yamamoto and his inspection team. This bold mission eliminated Japan's premier strategist and severely undermined Japanese morale.

By late 1943 both the 5th and 13th Air Forces were flying long-range missions in concert to Rabaul, eventually eliminating this bastion of enemy strength without the need for invasion. The effort went so well that the Solomons were also secured. In June 1944 both air forces were then put under a single command, the Far East Air Force, with all aircraft flying from New Guinea, which was under Allied control by July.

Long-range strikes to Halmahera Islands softened the area for the invasion of September 1944, and 835 mile round trip bombing missions covered by P–38s were flown to the oil refineries on Balikpapan, Borneo. With the Allied invasion of the Philippines in October, American fighter pilots were constantly opposed while protecting the ground forces. The numbers of Japanese aircraft destroyed, particularly by P–38s and P–47s, climbed rapidly until the Japanese ran out of people and planes. The first P–51s appeared in the theater with the 3rd Air Commando Group in late December, led by such experienced ETO pilots as Bud Mahurin. By the spring of 1945 the 35th and 348th Groups were flying Mustangs.

With little in the way of enemy aircraft to find, the fighter pilots spent more time in ground support, though aerial combat was common during the long-range missions into Southeast Asia and Formosa. By late June, the 5th AF moved its fighter units to Okinawa for the invasion of Japan, but in August 1945 the dropping of two atomic bombs ended the war.

The 5th Air Force produced 147 aces, most of them having gained their kills in the P–38. Thomas McGuire was behind Bong at thirty-eight while 475th Group CO Charles McDonald got twenty-seven. Though the large P–47 was not considered the best fighter to go against the nimble Japanese, 348th Group CO Neel E. Kearby shot down twenty-two aircraft before being killed in the middle of a dogfight. Often in places where less action took place, the 13th Air Force had twenty-three fighter aces, with P–38 pilots again dominating the rankings. Robert W. Westbrook had twenty victories, Bill Harris had sixteen and C. B. Head had twelve.

Not until mid 1944 did the 7th Air Force, which had been formed from the units under attack at Pearl Harbor, begin to see intensive combat. With the invasion of Saipan, two squadrons of the 318th Fighter Group flew their P–47s off escort carriers to the island, and by July it was fully operational. Though the Thunderbolts were effective in the Marianas and Iwo Jima, they did not have the range to be effective on the long over-water fighter operations that were necessary in the Pacific theater. As a result, P–38s were transferred from Hawaii to the group and the unit's first victories were scored.

After B–29s started flying from Saipan and Tinian in late 1944, Iwo Jima was invaded in February 1945 to provide a base for escort fighters and for Superfortress emergency landings. Both the 15th and 21st Fighter Groups flew in with their P–51Ds and the 506th Group arrived in April. By July the 414th Fighter Group arrived with long-range P–47Ns. The first long-range escort mission to Japan was flown by the 15th and 21st Groups in April, bringing the Japanese Home Defense fighters up in

Japanese Zeke being shot down by a Navy F6F Hellcat. Flame and smoke nearly obscure the whole left wing of the Zeke, heading into the deep six. *National Archives, via Kevin Grantham*

A bitter harvest for this Japanese pilot and crew as smoke is seen coming from its engine and rear gun position. *MAFB*

great numbers, something that would continue until the end of the war. With round trip distances of 1,500 miles taking up to ten hours, these missions were tough on pilots who had to sit on seat pack parachutes in a small cockpit.

The 7th Air Force's 318th Group was assigned to the 20th Air Force to fly long range escort in P–47Ns from Ie Shima along with two other similarly equipped groups. Between May 1945 and the surrender in August, several Thunderbolt pilots became aces in the wild air battles over Japan. A total of twelve aces were produced by the 7th Air Force, four having become aces on a single mission. The 15th Group's Robert W. Moore (12.5 kills) and John W. Mitchell (three of eleven kills while with the 15th) led the way.

The heat, humidity, tents, voracious insects and tropical diseases of the Pacific took their human toll but they did not stop US fighter pilots from destroying a fiercely determined enemy. That these men kept their sense of humor and their dreams of home is borne out by the art they painted on their aircraft.

Although many of these Japanese aircraft are hidden under the trees, they have been spotted and are the target of parafrag bombing. *MAFB*

RUFF STUFF, a P–38 piloted by Capt. Norbert C. Ruff of the 80th Fighter Squadron, 8th Fighter Group, 5th Air Force. Capt. Ruff is credited with five aerial victories.

HELL FROM HEAVEN, P–38 piloted by 1st Lt. William "Patty" W. Turner, 36th Fighter Squadron, 8th Fighter Group. Notice the flurry of arrows shot from the harp. Lt. Turner is credited with three aerial victories. P–38 *National Association, via Joe Kuhn*

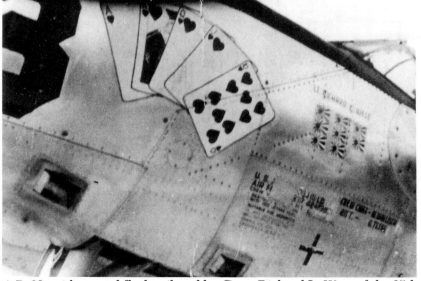

A P–38, with a royal flush, piloted by Capt. Richard L. West of the 35th Fighter Squadron, 8th Fighter Group. Capt. West is credited with fourteen aerial victories. *Jeff Ethell*

PORKY II, a P–38 piloted by Maj. Edward Cragg of the 80th Fighter Squadron, 8th Fighter Group. Maj. Cragg is credited with fifteen aerial victories. *Jeff Ethell*

Itchy Triggers, a P–38 of the 80th Fighter Squadron, 8th Fighter Group. *AFM*

PAY OFF, a P–38 piloted by Lt. M. M. Jarboe of the 8th Fighter Group. *Crow*

Miss Polly, a P–38 of the 8th Fighter Group. *Crow*

WISHFUL THINKING, a P–38 of the 8th Fighter Group. *Crow*

A P–38 of the 8th Fighter Group. *Crow*

AIR A CUTIE, a P39F of the 36th Fighter Squadron, 8th Fighter Group, New Guinea, 1943.

Glamour-Puss II, a P-38 of the 80th Fighter Squadron, 8th Fighter Group. *Hickey, via Crow*

Jean Creamer, a P-38 of the 80th Fighter Squadron, 8th Fighter Group. *Hickey, via Crow*

A P-38 piloted by Capt. Paul C. Murphey, Jr., of the 80th Fighter Squadron, 8th Fighter Group. Capt. Murphey is credited with six aerial victories. *Jeff Ethell*

HALF PINT, more Disney-inspired nose art on a P-38 piloted by 1st Lt. Russell M. Roth of the 80th Fighter Squadron, 8th Fighter Group. Roth is credited with two aerial victories. *Saffro, via Crow*

LIL-DE-ICER, a P-38 of the 80th Fighter Squadron, 8th Fighter Group. Photo taken in New Guinea, 1943. *Saffro, via Crow*

DEVIL ANSE II, a P-38 piloted by Lt. Hugh L. Hatfield of the 80th Fighter Squadron, 8th Fighter Group. The hillbilly nose art alludes to the "Hatfields and McCoys". *Saffro, via Crow*

A P–38 piloted by Lt. S. King of the 8th Fighter Group. *Kleist, via Crow*

G. I. Miss U, nose art from the 35th Fighter Squadron, 8th Fighter Group. *Hickey, via Crow*

Vagrant Virgin, a P–38 piloted by Lt. L. V. Bellusel of the 36th Fighter Squadron, 8th Fighter Group. *Saffro, via Crow*

Jandina IV, a P–38 piloted by Maj. Jay T. Robbins of the 80th Fighter Squadron, 8th Fighter Group. Robbins scored twenty-two aerial victories. The aircraft name is a combination of "Jay," "and" and his wife's name "Ina." This is the last of four aircraft named *Jandina*.

CHICAGO KID, a P–38 piloted by 1st Lt. Jack A. Ericsson of the 36th Fighter Squadron, 8th Fighter Group. *P–38 National Association, via Joe Kuhn*

Dorothy Marie, MY PET, a P–38 piloted by Lt. J. Dixon of the 8th Fighter Group. He is pictured here with his Crew Chief S/Sgt. Essen. Photo taken at Ie Shima, 1945. *Kleist, via Crow*

Ruby Don't you just Lo-o-ove These Cushions, the engine cowling art is from *Dorothy Marie, MY PET. Kleist, via Crow*

X Virgin, a P–38 piloted by Capt. Kenneth G. Ladd of the 80th Fighter Squadron, 8th Fighter Group. This nose art is inspired by the artwork of Alberto Vargas. Ladd is credited with twelve aerial victories, the last two on October 14, 1944, after he transferred to the 36th Fighter Squadron. Photo taken in New Guinea, September 1943. *Saffro, via Crow*

Windy City Ruthie, another P–38 piloted by Capt. Kenneth G. Ladd. *Windy City Ruthie* was named for the wife of Crew Chief Yale Saffro from Chicago, Illinois. *Saffro, via Crow*

A P–38 of the 80th Fighter Squadron, 8th Fighter Group. *Hickey, via Crow*

HILL'S ANGELS, a P–38J piloted by Capt. Allen E. Hill of the 80th Fighter Squadron, 8th Fighter Group. Hill is credited with nine aerial victories. *Saffro, via Crow*

Opposite side of *HILL'S ANGELS,* showing the second of the angels and Walt Disney's Dopey. *Saffro, via Crow*

A P–38 piloted by Capt. R. I. Meinhard of the 8th Fighter Group. *Crow*

Ready Maid, a P–38 of the 80th Fighter Squadron, 8th Fighter Group. *Hickey, via Crow*

A P–38 of the 8th Fighter Group. *Kleist, via Crow*

A P–38 of the 36th Fighter Squadron, 8th Fighter Group. Note the "Flying Fiend" on the nose, the insignia of the 36th Fighter Squadron. *Kleist, via Crow*

G.I. Virgin, a P–38, group and squadron unknown, however it was a member of the 13th Fighter Command, 8th Air Force. The picture was taken on Rykyo, Okinawa, 1945. *AFM*

A P-47 piloted by 2nd Lt. William D. Ray, Jr., of the 78th Fighter Squadron, 15th Fighter Group. The 15th was stationed in Hawaii and suffered numerous casualties when Pearl Harbor was attacked. *MAFB*

A P-47 piloted by 1st Lt. Victor J. Wahl of the 47th Fighter Squadron, 15th Fighter Group. Wahl earned two Battle Stars, an Air Medal and a DFC. *MAFB*

STINGEREE, a P-47 piloted by 2nd Lt. George R. Duncan of the 15th Fighter Group. *MAFB*

HOT NUTS, a P-47 piloted by 2nd Lt. Lee J. Blanchard of the 78th Fighter Squadron, 15th Fighter Group. *MAFB*

MISS AMBER, art on the gun doors of the P-38 piloted by "Coffee" Coffman of the 12th Fighter Squadron, 18th Fighter Group, 13th Air Force. *MISS AMBER* was painted by Coffee. Photo taken at Camp Zamboanga, Philippines. P-38 *National Association, via Joe Kuhn*

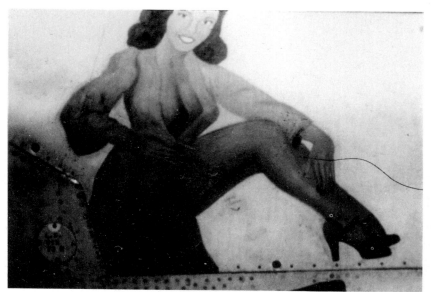

The starboard gun panel installed on *MISS AMBER*, a P–38 piloted by "Coffee" Coffman. *Col. William Fowkes*

HEADY HEDY, a P–38 of the 18th Fighter Group. In the long hours of over-water flight this pilot had plenty of time to daydream about starlet Hedy Lamar. *Col. William Fowkes*

"*HAWKEYE HATTIE-II*", a P–38 of the 18th Fighter Group. *Col. William Fowkes*

Hell's Angel, a P–38 of the 18th Fighter Group. *Col. William Fowkes*

Little ANGEL, a P–38 of the 18th Fighter Group. *Col. William Fowkes*

PHILLIE BABY II, a P–38 of the 18th Fighter Group. *Col. William Fowkes*

A P-38 with a very stylish rooster pulling a wagon. The number 400 on the nose identifies the aircraft as a member of the 18th Fighter Group, 13th Air Force. *Kita, via Crow*

Lander 3715, a P-38 of the 18th Fighter Group. *Col. William Fowkes*

Sweet Sybil, a P-38 of the 18th Fighter Group. *Col. William Fowkes*

Pacific Prowler, a P-38 piloted by Lt. Clint Ward of the 44th Fighter Squadron, 18th Fighter Group. This nose art shows an excellent caricature of the P-38. His Crew Chief was Sgt. C. Baudenbush. *Paul Fournet*

An artist's sketch of the P-38, *Pacific Prowler. Clint Ward*

Lt. Joe D. Barbee's P–38, 12th Fighter Squadron, 18th Fighter Group. 2nd Lt. Tommy Caldwell painted this from an Air Force poster which said, "Are your PIPS showing? turn on your IFF identification." This pin-up art comes with a good story. Caldwell was returning from a strike on the Balikpapan oil fields in Borneo when he was forced to bail out along the Zulu Archipelago. He drifted 250 miles in 10 days in a one-man raft before he was washed up on the shore of Mindanao. The natives there nursed him back to health and notified the Navy. In about two weeks the Navy picked him up in a P.T. boat and returned him to Zamboanga. He painted this nose art while he was recuperating. *Lt. Joe D. Barbee*

"TEENA", a P–38 piloted by Lt. Col. Homer Tennant, 70th Fighter Squadron, 18th Fighter Group, named after Homer's wife, Loristeen. *Homer Tennant*

Baby Jay, a P–38 shown with Maj. John R. Mulvey, CO of the 12th Fighter Squadron, 18th Fighter Group. Photo taken at Zamboanga, Philippines, 1945. *Homer Tennant*

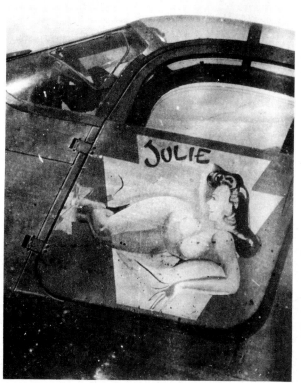

JULIE, a P–39 Airacobra, group and squadron unknown. *MAFM*

Billy's Filly, a P–38 piloted by Col. William Fowkes of the 12th Fighter Squadron, 18th Fighter Group. Picture taken early in 1945, Zamboanga, Philippines. *Col. William Fowkes*

SPARE PARTS, a P–39 of the 46th Fighter Squadron, 21st Fighter Group, 7th Air Force. This P–39 was reconstructed from a condemned airframe to become the fastest in the Pacific. Notice the "?" on the tail in place of a number. *E. McDowell*

Tarawa Boom De-Ay, a P–39Q–1, (s/n 42–19549) piloted by Maj. Joseph H. Powell of the 72nd Fighter Squadron, 21st Fighter Group. *AFM*

A P–51 assigned to the 46th Fighter Squadron, 21st Fighter Group. *Donald Theime*

Rudder art from a P–40, group and squadron unknown. *Jerry McKee*

A P–39, piloted by Maj. William McDonough of the 40th Fighter Squadron, 35th Fighter Group. McDonough was killed in a parachute jump while awaiting transportation to return him to the States. McDonough was credited with five aerial victories. *MAFB*

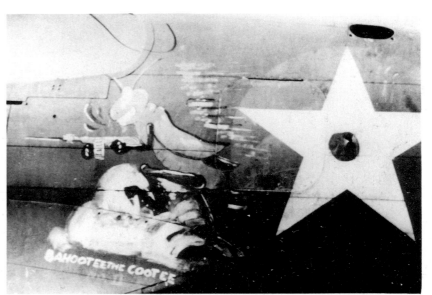

BAHOOTEE THE COOTEE No. II, a P–40 piloted by Lt. Robert F. McMahon of the 39th Fighter Squadron, 35th Fighter Group. Nose art shows a machine gun wielding cootee. Lt. McMahon is credited with one aerial victory. *E. McDowell*

"KISS ME", one of the first Mustangs used by the 35th Fighter Group. Transition to the new fighter began early in March, 1945. In its long history in the theater, the 35th used four different types of fighter aircraft: P–38s, P–39s, P–47s and P–51s. *MAFB*

"MACUSHLA," a P-63 King Cobra of the 35th Pursuit Group has the beginnings of a shark mouth on the nose of the aircraft. Note the Donald Duck door art.

The C–47 *Swamp Rat* of the 6th Troop Corkler Squadron is being escorted to a drop zone in New Guinea by two sets of Airacobras from the 35th Fighter Group. *USAF, via E. McDowell*

JAPANESE SANDMAN II, a P–38 piloted by Lt. Richard Eugene "Snuffy" Smith of the 39th Fighter Squadron, 35th Fighter Group. Smith is credited with seven aerial victories. *P–38 National Association, via Joe Kuhn*

JAPANESE SANDMAN II, as it appeared in 1986, with "Snuffy" Smith once again in the pilot's seat. After Snuffy was rotated, the plane crashed on takeoff. When he learned that David Pennifather, a WWII memorabilia collector, had located the plane, he and his wife Dorothy took the trip to reunite pilot and plane. The plane was not recoverable but an old friend and old memories were revisited. *via Joe Kuhn*

"STAR DUST"/OKLAHOMA-KID, a P-40 piloted by Lt. Andrew J. Reynolds of the 9th Fighter Squadron, 49th Fighter Group, 5th Air Force. Lt. Reynolds is credited with ten aerial victories. *AFM*

"STAR DUST"/OKLAHOMA-KID, the starboard cowling of the P-40 piloted by Lt. Andrew J. Reynolds of the 9th Fighter Squadron, 49th Fighter Group. Lt. Reynolds scored four victories while serving the 17th Pursuit Squadron in Java and another six with the 49th. *AFM*

Dopey, a P-47 piloted by Lt. James A. Posten of the 9th Squadron of the 49th Fighter Group. Posten is credited with three confirmed aerial victories. *E. McDowell*

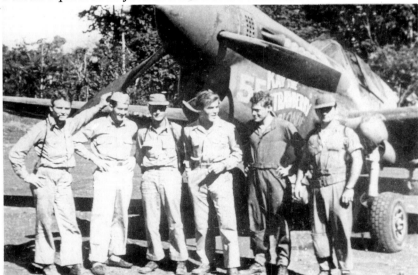

KAY THE STRAWBERRY BLONDE, a P-40E (s/n 41-367153) piloted by Lt. Sammy A. Pierce of the 8th Fighter Squadron, 49th Fighter Group. Lt. Pierce is credited with seven aerial victories.

Bigasburd, a P-47 piloted by Lt. Howard R. Oglesby of the 9th Fighter Squadron, 49th Fighter Group. Oglesby scored four aerial victories. *E. McDowell*

Little Rebel, a P39Q, was the first plane to use the reconquered air strip on Mabin Island in the Gilberts. Note the spiral striping on the gun barrels. Also note the beginnings of a cobra on the engine cowlings. *via E. McDowell*

GEORGIA BELLE, a P–38 flown by Capt. Joel B. Paris of the 7th Squadron, 49th Fighter Group. Paris is credited with nine aerial victories. *E. McDowell*

My Marie, a P–38 piloted by Capt. Fred Dick of the 7th Fighter Squadron, 49th Fighter Group. Capt. Dick is credited with five aerial victories.

A P–40 of the 7th Fighter Squadron, 49th Fighter Group. *E. McDowell*

Winnie, a P–38 of the 49th Fighter Group. *Winnie* was assigned to Lt. Costley. *E. McDowell*

"SCATTER BRAIN", a P–40 piloted by Lt. Edgar D. Ball of the 7th Fighter Squadron, 49th Fighter Group. This plane was named after a song that was popular at this time. A crewman is cleaning off the oil from one of the Zeroes that Ball shot down. *Jeff Ethell*

STEW HEAD IV, a P–40 of the 7th Fighter Squadron, 49th Fighter Group. *AFM*

TYPHOON McGOON, a P-40 flown by Lt. Clyde V. Knisley of the 7th Fighter Squadron, 49th Fighter Group, before the name was painted. *E. McDowell*

TYPHOON McGOON with the name added to the nose art. *E. McDowell*

ANA MAY, a P-40E piloted by Capt. Melson D. Flack, Jr. of the 8th Fighter Squadron, 49th Fighter Group. Flack scored five aerial victories. Note the eagle over crossed American flags. *E. McDowell*

"GYPSY", a P-38L flown by Lt. K. B. Clark of the 9th Fighter Squadron, 49th Fighter Group while in the Philippines. Note the diving girl on the shield. *via E. McDowell*

Swing it, a P-40E piloted by Lt. Donald H. Lee, Jr., of the 7th Fighter Squadron, 49th Fighter Group. Photo taken at Port Moresby, New Guinea, mid-1943. Lt. Lee has four confirmed aerial victories. *E. McDowell*

Squirlbate, a P-40E of the 85th Fighter Squadron, 49th Fighter Group flown by Lt. Richard J. Vodra in New Guinea during 1943. Lt. Vodra has two confirmed victories. *via E. McDowell*

Beautiful Lass, a P-38G (s/n 43-2204) piloted by John G. "Jump" O'Neill of the 9th Fighter Squadron, 49th Fighter Group. O'Neill has eight aerial victories to his credit. *E. McDowell*

POOPY II, a P-40E (s/n 42-85396) piloted by Lt. A. T. House, Jr., of the 7th Fighter Squadron, 49th Fighter Group. Lt. House is credited with four confirmed victories and one aircraft damaged. *USAF, via E. McDowell*

EAGLEBEAK, a P-40E piloted by Capt. John C. Selman, who later became CO of the 49th, is pictured here testing his guns at Darwin, Australia in August, 1942. Note eight point stars on the wheel hubs.

THE SPODDESSAPE, a P-40E piloted by Lt. Randall D. Keator of the 8th Squadron, 49th Fighter Group. Keator downed two Zeroes while assigned to the 20th Pursuit Squadron flying a P-40B. *Pierce, via E. McDowell*

SKEETER, a P-40E flown by Lt. John D. Landers. This was Lander's first aircraft. The nose art shows a diving mosquito, armed with a tommy gun. *A. J. Reynolds, via E. McDowell*

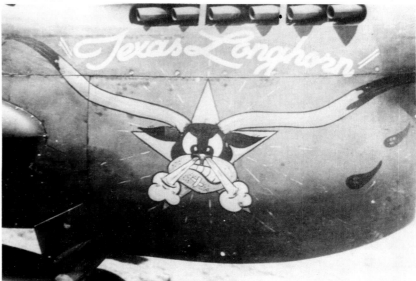

"Texas Longhorn", another P-40E (s/n 41-25164) piloted by Lt. John D. Landers. Landers is credited with six aerial victories in the Southwest Pacific. He also scored 8.5 victories in the ETO while flying the P-51D *Big Beautiful Doll*. *E. McDowell*

This P-38L (s/n 44-25916) was piloted by Maj. J. R. Petrovich of the 9th Fighter Squadron, 49th Fighter Group. The insignia on the nose is based on the 9th Squadron's "Flying Knights" helmet insignia. *USAAF, via E. McDowell*

This P-47 piloted by Capt. Ralph H. "Ironass" Wandrey of the 9th Fighter Squadron, 49th Fighter Group. Capt. Wandrey has six confirmed victories and two probables. Note the bathing beauty holding what appears to be a spyglass. *Wandrey, via E. McDowell*

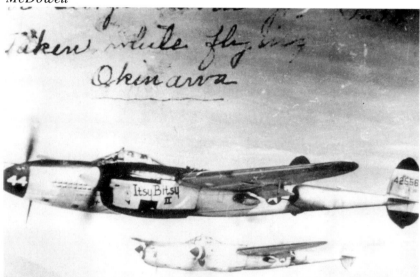

Itsy Bitsy II, a P-38 flown by Maj. George Laven, Jr. of the 49th Fighter Group showing a portion of the seventeen locomotives he destroyed. The photo shows a lot of black trim (not decoration) used to cover up patches resulting from repair of combat damage. *E. McDowell*

Empty Saddle, a P-40 piloted by Maj. Arland Stanton of the 7th Fighter Squadron, 49th Fighter Group. The port side carried the name *Keystone Katie*. Maj. Stanton is credited with eight aerial victories. *Sorci, via Crow*

O'Riley's Daughter, a P-40 piloted by 1st Lt. Jack Fenimore of the 7th Fighter Squadron, 49th Fighter Group. Lt. Fenimore is credited with one aerial victory, on May 15, 1944. *AFM*

"Milk Wagon Express", a P-40 of the 49th Fighter Group. *Sorcia, via Crow*

"Scarlet Night", a P-40N, assigned to the Headquarters Flight of the 49th Fighter Group, Philippine Islands, 1944. *Vitacco, via Crow*

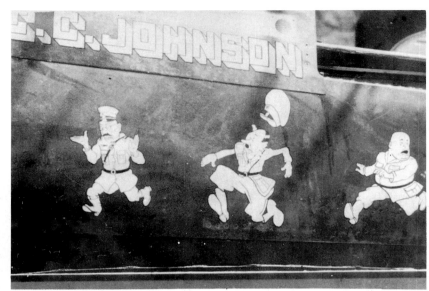

Maybelle, a P-40E piloted by Capt. Charles C. Johnson, III, of the 8th Fighter Squadron, 49th Fighter Group. This art, Tojo, Hitler and Mussolini on the run, is painted on the port side below the windscreen. *Maybelle* is painted on the nose. *Sims, via Crow*

BUCKET O' BOLTS, a P-40 of the 7th Fighter Squadron, 49th Fighter Group. *Vitacco, via Crow*

Pop's Blue Ribbon, a P-40 piloted by Capt. Paul J. Slocum, 7th Fighter Squadron, 49th Fighter Group. Slocum scored two aerial victories. The first was on November 22, 1942, and the second July 3, 1943. *Vitacco, via Crow*

Dawn Patrol, a P-40 assigned to the Headquarters Flight of the 49th Fighter Group. Photo taken in New Guinea, 1944. *Vitacco, via Crow*

"MARY LOU", a P-40 piloted by Lt. David R. Winternitz of the 8th Fighter Squadron, 49th Fighter Group. Lt. Winternitz scored one aerial victory on February 14, 1944. *AFM*

A P-40 of the 7th Fighter Squadron, 49th Fighter Group. *Vitacco, via Crow*

TARHEEL, a P-40E piloted by Lt. George Preddy. This aircraft carries the nickname that natives of North Carolina (Preddy's home state) are known by. *E. McDowell*

The dragon on the starboard side of Lt. George Preddy's *TARHEEL*. Preddy transferred to the 352nd Fighter Group in the ETO and scored 26.8 aerial victories against the Germans. *via E. McDowell*

Capt. Clay Tice, Jr., of the 9th Fighter Squadron, 49th Fighter Group in front of his P-40E in the summer of 1942. Capt. Tice has two confirmed aerial victories. Note the tomahawk behind the skull. *via E. McDowell*

Elsie, a P-38J piloted by Lt. Col. Clay Tice, Jr. Tice was CO of the 49th Fighter Group and is credited with two aerial victories. *via E. McDowell*

Another photo of *ELSIE* showing the skull and tomahawk artwork carried over from Tice's P-40. *E. McDowell*

L'Ace, a P-40 of the 7th Fighter Squadron, 49th Fighter Group. *L'Ace* was piloted by Capt. James B. Morehead. Morehead shot down two planes while with the 17th Pursuit Squadron, five while with the 49th and one with the 1st Fighter Group in Italy. *Francella, via Crow*

DONT WORRY!/*Bluebeard II*, a P-40E piloted by Lt. P. L. Alford of the 49th Fighter Group. On the starboard side is a silk worm carrying a caterpillar club membership card for "hitting the silk." The port side carried the name *Bluebeard II*. E. McDowell

ARIZONA, a P-40 piloted by Maj. Sidney S. Woods of the 9th Fighter Squadron, 49th Fighter Group. Coiled by a cactus plant is an excited rattlesnake. Woods is credited with two aerial victories. E. McDowell

The slightly different rattlesnake on the starboard side of *ARIZONA*. *E. McDowell*

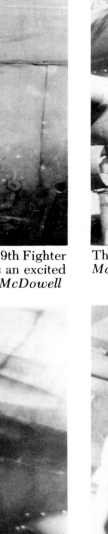

The Little Virgin, a P-40 piloted by Lt. William A. Levitan of the 9th Fighter Squadron, 49th Fighter Group. Levitan was killed in an accident on March 3, 1943. He is credited with two aerial victories. E. McDowell

A P-40 piloted by Capt. George Kiser of the 8th Fighter Squadron, 49th Fighter Group. The artwork shows a lion holding a Japanese pilot in his right paw and crushing a Zero under its left paw. Kiser is credited with nine aerial victories. E. McDowell

A P–40 piloted by Capt. Robert M. DeHaven of the 7th Fighter Squadron, 49th Fighter Group. DeHaven chose the orchid as his personal insignia and had it painted on all of his aircraft. He also chose No. 13 (his birthdate and lucky number) for his airplanes. *E. McDowell*

A P–38 piloted by Capt. Robert M. DeHaven, sporting a stylized orchid. The orchid has taken on the shape of an aircraft marked with "13". It is firing out of the front and carries USAAF markings on the pedals. Flying the orchid is a gremlin with pointed ears. *E. McDowell*

This P–38 piloted by Capt. DeHaven has the same flying orchid but the plane no longer has the number 13 on the nose. It has fourteen Japanese flags for his fourteen aerial victories. *E. McDowell*

Ragged But Right, a P–40 piloted by Lt. John Bodak of the 8th Fighter Squadron, 49th Fighter Group. Lt. Bodak is credited with three aerial victories. *E. McDowell*

Ragged But Right, a P–38 piloted by Lt. Bodak. This aircraft wears the same lady but she is no longer sitting on a blanket. *E. McDowell*

THE REBEL, a P–40E flown by Lt. Ben Irvin of the 9th Fighter Squadron, 49th Fighter Group. Irvin was known to his mates as "Bitchin Ben" and scored two aerial victories while assigned to the 17th Pursuit Squadron (provisional). *E. McDowell*

Grade A, a P-40 piloted by Capt. Elliott E. Dent, Jr. of the 7th Fighter Squadron, 49th Fighter Group. Capt. Elliott is credited with six aerial victories. *E. McDowell*

"SOUTHERN *Miss*", a P-38 piloted by Capt. Richard Ganchan (right) of the 7th Fighter Squadron, 49th Fighter Group. The painting is of Ganchan's wife and the artist was Lt. Robert Klemmedson. Pictured with Ganchan is Crew Chief Scully E. Voss. *E. McDowell*

"*Miss Kat*", a P-40 piloted by Lt. Lawrence N. Succop of the 7th Fighter Squadron, 49th Fighter Group. Pictured with "*Miss Kat*" is Capt. Ernie Harris, CO of the 8th Fighter Squadron. This picture was taken at Dobodura, New Guinea during 1943. *E. McDowell*

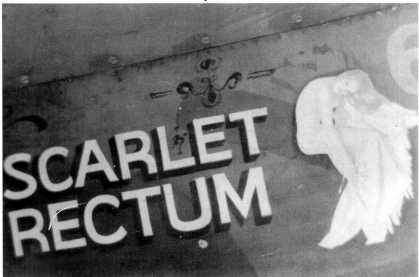

SCARLETT RECTUM, a P-40E piloted by Lt. William B. Harris of the 8th Fighter Squadron, 49th Fighter Group. Lt. Harris has three confirmed aerial victories. *E. McDowell*

Nita, a P-40 assigned to the 49th Fighter Group. *E. McDowell*

DADDY PLEASE, a P-40 assigned to the 7th Fighter Squadron, 49th Fighter Group. The artwork of the 49th was some of the more risque found during World War II. *E. McDowell*

DUCK BUTT, a P-40E Warhawk flown by Lt. James A. "Duck Butt" Watkins of the 9th Fighter Squadron, 49th Fighter Group. Watkins earned his nickname from the way he walked when wearing a parachute. He destroyed one aircraft. *E. McDowell*

Charlcie Jeanne, a P-38L (s/n 44-26407) flown by Maj. James A. "Duck Butt" Watkins. Capt. Watkins piloted his way to eleven aerial victories in P-38s. *E. McDowell*

My Anxious Mama!, a P-40 piloted by Lt. Robert W. Croft of the 7th Fighter Squadron, 49th Fighter Group. *Sorci, via Crow*

Dorothy Mae, a P-40 piloted by Flight Officer Arthur L. Talmage of the 8th Fighter Squadron, 49th Fighter Group. Talmage is credited with one aerial victory, on April 12, 1943. *Crow*

Rosy Cheeks, a P-40 of the 7th Fighter Squadron, 49th Fighter Group. *Vitacco, via Crow*

EMBRACEABLE YOU, a P-48L of the 9th Fighter Squadron, 49th Fighter Group, flown by Lt. Edward B. Howes. Howes, scored a total of four aerial victories. Sgt. Belwan the squadron painter is on the left and Howes is on the right. *E. McDowell*

The American Ace of Aces, Maj. Richard I. Bong, destroyed forty enemy aircraft, confirmed, damaged seven, and had eight unconfirmed kills. During his three combat tours with the 49th, Bong was awarded the Congressional Medal of Honor, the DFC, DSC, Air Medal with clusters and the Silver Star. He was killed in the explosion of a P-80A jet fighter on August 6, 1945. *MAFB*

Almost "a" Draggin, a P-38L piloted by Maj. Clayton M. Isaacson of the 7th Fighter Squadron, 49th Fighter Group. He started fighting in the MTO, racking up two Me 109s and one Me 210 destroyed, 1.5 Me 109s damaged, and a probable on an Fw 190. *Vitacco, via Crow*

ALMOST "A" DRAGGIN II another P-38L piloted by Maj. Isaacson.

Cro. Bait, a P-38 flown by Fred C. Beach of the 8th Fighter Squadron, 49th Fighter Group. *Crow*

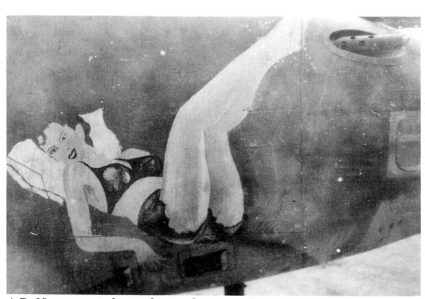

A P-38, group and squadron unknown. The coloring and numbering is similar to some in the 49th Fighter Group. *Crow*

Texas Baby, a P-40N assigned to the 8th Fighter Squadron, 49th Fighter Group. No. 43 has its own version of the artwork known as "Pistol Packin Mama". *E. McDowell*

Barbara, a P-38 piloted by Lt. Col. Gerald R. Johnson, the 49th Fighter Group ace for whom Johnson Army Air Base is named. Johnson started his fighter pilot career by completing fifty-eight missions with the 57th Fighter Squadron in Alaska. In the Southwest Pacific, he scored twenty-two confirmed victories and nineteen probables. *MAFB*

A P-40E piloted by Lt. J. A. Angel of the 9th Fighter Squadron, 49th Fighter Group, sporting an angel with a machine gun. *Betty Whittly*

Island Dream, a P-40N of the 7th Fighter Squadron, 49th Fighter Group. *E. McDowell*

On the tail of this P-38 is the 7th Fighter Squadron's Bunyap insignia. It also wears the red and white rudder stripes which the 7th used late in the war. *E. McDowell*

LiL' JO, a P-38 piloted by Lt. James Haislip, Jr. of the 9th Fighter Squadron, 49th Fighter Group. The wolf dressed in top hat and tails has a red lightning bolt behind his head with a blue circular background. *E. McDowell*

"DOLLYE", a P-40E flown by Lt. Eisenbury of the 8th Fighter Squadron, 49th Fighter Group. Behind the cockpit is a female Sagittarius or Centaur. *E. McDowell*

A P–39D (s/n 41–7341) bearing the wolf's head, the unofficial insignia of the 57th Fighter Squadron, 54th Fighter Group, 11th Air Force. This group fought in the Aleutians and received a DUC for its operations from June to November of 1942. *AFM*

Miss Mary Lou, a P–47 piloted by Maj. Henry McAfee of the 318th Fighter Group, 7th Air Force. *AFM*

MAD RUSSIAN, a P–47 of the 318th Fighter Group, 7th Air Force. *Rick McGowen*

Some Punkins, a P–47 of the 73rd Fighter Squadron, 318th Fighter Group. *Rick McGowen*

Millie, a P–47 of the 318th Fighter Group. *Rick McGowen*

Dream Gal, a P–47 of the 318th Fighter Group. *Rick McGowen*

Shack RABBIT, a P-47, possibly of the 333rd Fighter Squadron, 318th Fighter Group. *AFM*

2 BIG and Too HEAVY, a P-47 of the 333rd Fighter Squadron, 318th Fighter Group. Note the Squadron insignia under the cockpit. *Tucker, via Crow*

WICKED WEE, a P-47 of the 333rd Fighter Squadron, 318th Fighter Group. *O'Rourke, via Crow*

SHORT SNORTER, a P-47 of the 318th Fighter Group. *Witte, via Crow*

Glori Gal, a P-47 of the 73rd Fighter Squadron, 318th Fighter Group. *Hickey, via Crow*

DAN'L BOONE, a P-47 of the 333rd Fighter Squadron, 318th Fighter Group. Photo taken at Kagman Field, Saipan. *AFM*

I'VE HAD IT, a P–47 of the 318th Fighter Group. Photo taken on Ie Shima, in August, 1945. *Tucker, via Crow*

Ripper II, a P–38 of the 333rd Fighter Squadron, 318th Fighter Group. Note that the carrot looks like Tojo. *O'Rouke, via Crow*

Artwork found its way from the noses of aircraft to the tails and any place in between. Note the message on the bomb hung on this P–47, piloted by Lt. Col. Harry McAfee. *Crow*

The starboard side of *I'VE HAD IT*. It's clearly the same artist, but the girls are different. *Tucker, via Crow*

SACK HAPPY, a P–47 of the 318th Fighter Group. *Rick McGowen*

Itchy Bitch, a P–38J–10–LO piloted by Lt. Eustis of the 333rd Fighter Squadron, 318th Fighter Group. Lt. Eustis was shot down in this plane over Truk on January 14, 1945, and was taken prisoner by the Japanese. *Joseph Maita via Warren Bodie*

Mighty Mad, an A–26 of the 319th Bombardment Group. In April through July of 1945, the group was stationed in Okinawa and flew missions to Japan and China, attacking airfields, shipping, and other targets. *Neal and Nina Baker*

A P–40, piloted by Maj. John Chennault of the 11th Fighter Squadron, 343rd Fighter Group, stationed in the Aleutians. The group adopted the "Aleutian Tiger" as a tribute to Chennault's father Claire Chennault's Flying Tigers." *USAF*

A P–40 of the 343rd Fighter Group based on Kisha, September, 1942. The painting of the Bengal was a tribute to their commanding officer Maj. John Chennault. Maj. Chennault was the son of General Chennault. *E. McDowell*

A P–40 of the 18th Fighter Squadron, 343rd Fighter Group, in the Aleutians. The Blue Foxes expressed their feelings for the enemy in this work of art showing Pluto paying his respects to the Japanese rising sun. *E. McDowell*

A P–40 with interesting artwork, group and squadron unknown. *Donnie Watts*

Si Si Señor, a P–38 of the 347th Fighter Group, 13th Air Force. *MAFB*

FRAIDY KAT, a P–38 (s/n 44–26388) of the 347th Fighter Group. *Willet*

SHOOT! YOU'RE FADED, a P–38 (s/n 44–25848) of the 68th Fighter Squadron, 347th Fighter Group.

IMPATIENT VIRGIN, a P–40 assigned to the 67th Fighter Squadron, 347th Fighter Group. Note the interesting shark mouth design. *E. McDowell*

TOJO, EAT SHIT, a P–38 of the 347th Fighter Group. *Homer Tennant*

MISS VIRGINITY, NEVER BEEN PLUGGED OR FORCED DOWN, a P–47 piloted by 1st Lt. James M. Nixon of the 341st Fighter Squadron, 348th Fighter Group, 5th Air Force. *Vitacco, via Crow*

A P–47 piloted by Major Bill Dunham of the 342nd and 460th Fighter Squadrons, 348th Fighter Group. Dunham scored sixteen aerial victories and sunk two cargo ships. *B. Hess*

DIRTY OLD MAN 4TH, a P–47 piloted by Maj. Walter G. Benz, Jr., of the 342nd Fighter Squadron, 348th Fighter Group. Benz is credited with eight aerial victories. *Pearsall, via Crow*

"PUTT PUTT MARU", a P–38 piloted by Col. Charles H. MacDonald CO of the 475th Fighter Group. The first PUTT PUTT MARU was a P–47 followed by four P–38s. *Jeff Ethell*

MacDonald's first P–38 named PUTT-PUTT MARU showing eight victory flags. *via J. Alexander*

Another *PUTT PUTT MARU* —with eleven victory flags. MacDonald (left) is shown with Charles Lindbergh—assigned to the 475th to show them how to get maximum range out of their P–38s. Note the "Satan's Angel" insignia on the tip of the P–38's nose. *via J. Alexander*

A P–38, showing the 431st Fighter Squadron emblem. Standing next to the plane is 1st Lt. Christopher J. Herman, a member of the 431st, credited with one aerial victory. Lt. Herman was killed in an A–26 at Haneda Air Force Base after the war. *Jeff Ethell*

VIRGINIA MARIE, a P–38J–15–LO, piloted by Lt. Bob Anderson of the 433rd Fighter Squadron, 475th Fighter Group. *AFM*

PAPPY'S Birr-die, a P–38 of the 431st Fighter Squadron, 475th Fighter Group. Note the names "Helen" and "Bobby" on the port engine cowling. *AFM*

"Pistol Packin' Ma-Ma", a P–38G piloted by Lt. Wood D. Clodfelter of the 431st Fighter Squadron, 475th Fighter Group. The Japanese victory flag with the white background stands for the Lily twin-engined light bomber that he shot down on February 3, 1944. *David Aiken*

CAROL DEE, a P–38 of the 431st Fighter Squadron, 475th Fighter Group shows fourteen fighter victories credited to this aircraft. The crew chief was S/Sgt. M. J. Allen and the assistant crew chief was S. Cram. *David Aiken*

"Pudgy IV", piloted by Maj. Thomas B. McGuire, Jr., of the 431st Fighter Squadron, 475th Fighter Group—the "Satan's Angels". *Jeff Ethell*

"Pudgy V" another P–38 piloted by McGuire. He is credited with thirty-eight kills and was CO of the 431st squadron. Mac was killed on Jan. 7, 1945. *Warren Bodie*

Impossible Ince, a P–38 piloted by 1st Lt. James C. Ince of the 432nd Fighter Squadron, 475th Fighter Group. Ince is credited with six aerial victories. *Crow*

"Hold Everything", a P–38H piloted by Lt. Paul V. Morriss of the 431st Fighter Squadron, 475th Fighter Group. Morriss destroyed a Zeke, a Val and three Oscars. *David Aiken*

Another view of *"Hold Everything"* with Lt. Paul Morriss. Morriss' crew chief was M. B. Russell and the assistant c/c was Asher. *David Aiken*

Is This Trip Necessary?, a P–51 of the 506th Fighter Group, 12th Air Force, after crashing on the runway at North Field, Iwo Jima. *AFM*

The SHELL PUSHER, a P–47 piloted by Lt. Bob Forrest of the 507th Fighter Group. Pictured by the name is a cannon shell. *B. Hess*

Expected Goose, a P–47N of the 463rd Fighter Squadron, 507th Fighter Squadron, Ie Shima, 1945. *Hickey, via Crow*

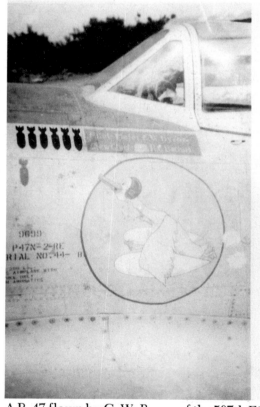

A P–47 flown by C. W. Byrne of the 507th Fighter Group at Ie Shima. *B. Hess*

An F6F Hellcat piloted by Lt. (jg) Alexander Vraciu of VF–6 (and later VF–16). Shown here with nine victories, he went on to become the Navy's fourth highest scoring fighter pilot with 19 confirmed kills.

Lt. Ira Kepford's F4U-1A Corsair in Bougainville, February 1944. This ship carries the skull and crossbones insignia of Tommy Blackburn's famous "Jolly Rogers" (VF-17). Kepford's aircraft displays sixteen of his seventeen confirmed aerial victories. *Warren Bodie*

A F6F Hellcat piloted by Capt. Terrance Rice of VF-21 landing on the carrier *Belleau Wood*. It wasn't a good landing, and, unfortunately, Capt. Rice didn't survive. Obscured by the wing is the shark mouth design on the cowl. *Jack Moses*

Edward Henry "Butch" O'Hare of VF-3 and VF-6 saved the USS *Lexington,* became the U.S. Navy's first ace and won the Congressional Medal of Honor on February 20, 1942, when he single-handedly attacked a wave of Japanese bombers, shooting down five and diverting the rest. In all, O'Hare scored twelve aerial victories before he was shot down and killed by the rear gunner on a Japanese bomber on November 26, 1943. *OASM*

An F4U-4 Corsair based at Iwo Jima. Pictured with the aircraft is Machinist Mate Donald Theime. *Donald Theime*

Beetle Bomb, an F8F-1 Bearcat that flew with the Blue Angels. 1949 was the one year the Blue Angels painted their aircraft yellow with blue lettering. They also switched to jets later in 1949. The team commander was Lt. Cdr. Dusty Rhodes. *Warren Bodie*

MARIE ELLER II and *FLORIDA GATOR*, a pair of TBM Avengers, both assigned to USS *Cape Glouchester* in 1945. *Jack Moses*

171

Another exception to the rules, this rare shot reveals a little humor with the angry eyed grimacing Hellcat. *B. Hess*

Polecat, an F6F Hellcat which broke in half as it landed on the carrier *Hancock* after a mission over Luzon. Notice the very small name and unit insignia, confirming that some Navy pilots were allowed to decorate their planes. *National Archives via Kevin Grantham*

Col. Gregory "Pappy" Boyington of the USMC, a wild, hard drinking, professional flyer from his days in the AVG (six victories) to the Marine Air VMF 214 Squadron (22 victories), was one of the most unconventional heroes of World War II.

Commander David McCampbell, a Navy ace with over thirty Japanese aircraft destroyed to his credit smiles from the cockpit of his F6F Hellcat aboard the USS *Essex.* McCampbell earned the Congressional Medal of Honor for destroying nine Japanese planes in one mission. *National Archives via Kevin Grantham*

CHINA DOLL, a P-38 piloted by Frank J. Dutko. The picture was taken at Howard Field, Panama, in 1945.

An F6F Hellcat after it nosed over upon landing on the USS *Hancock*, we see the pilot climbing out shaken but uninjured. Here again we see a small unit insignia yet not noticeable expanse of nose art. *National Archives via Kevin Grantham*

Commander McCampbell's *Minsi III*—an F6F Hellcat showing nineteen victories.

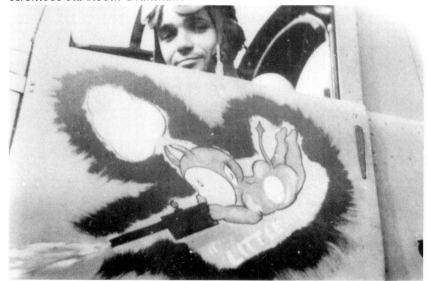

"*LITTLE DEVIL*", a P–39D assigned to the 13th Fighter Squadron, 53rd Fighter Group, stationed at Howard Field, Panama. The P–39's door made a good canvas for artwork. *E. McDowell*

MICKEY FINN ESQ, a P–39D piloted by Lt. Carter of the 13th Fighter Squadron, 53rd Fighter Group. Pictured on the door is a skull drinking from a wine glass. *E. McDowell*

A P–39 assigned to the 13th Fighter Squadron, 53rd Fighter Group. This pirate skeleton holds a flintlock pistol and a treasure map. A dagger pierces the center of a swastika. *E. McDowell*

A P–39 piloted by Lt. McNeill, assignment unknown. This is a trick picture. At first glance it is a bearded gentleman, but on closer observation you will notice the gentleman's nose is also the bent leg of a lady and his receding hair line is her torso. *E. McDowell*

173

"*No Love, NO NOTHIN II!*, a P-61 of the 422nd Night Fighter Squadron, 9th Air Force, 1944/45. *Crow*

Night Fighters

"Night fighting? It will never come to that!"—
Hermann Goring prophesied in 1939.

A year later both Britain and Germany were launching
night bombing raids against each other due to the heavy
losses they were taking in daylight. Existing fighters on
both sides were ineffective at night, even with the aid of
searchlights. Quite simply they could not find their targets.
The Bristol Beaufighter was the first aircraft powerful
enough to carry the new, heavy airborne intercept (AI)
radar, a pilot and radar operator, and heavy cannon
armament while maintaining a speed advantage for
pursuit of bombers. The deHavilland Mosquito was
quickly modified and it soon became the most effective
Allied night fighter of the war.

On the other side, the Germans soon had the
Messerschmitt 110 attacking the British bomber streams.
Though outclassed in many ways, the Bf 110 made aces of
many German pilots through the end of the war. By 1943
the night war was so massive the Germans had an
extensive network of fighter units flying Ju 88s and Do
217s as well. By the end the He 219, built solely for the
mission, was in action along with the jet propelled Me
262B and several special single engine units flying Bf 109s
and Fw 190s.

Following European trends carefully, the USAAF
ordered the Northrop P-61 Black Widow night fighter in
early 1941. When it was clear the aircraft would not be
available for the next few years, the Douglas A-20 Havoc
was modified and ordered as the P-70, a stop-gap to equip
the new night fighter squadrons awaiting the Black
Widow.

In mid 1943 the first four AAF night fighter squadrons
became operational with the 12th Air Force in the
Mediterranean. Though the P-70 carried an AI radar and
effective armament, it was underpowered for pursuit
operations, particularly at medium and high altitudes. The
414th, 415th, 416th and 417th Night Fighter Squadrons
(NFS) were able to re-equip with reverse lend-lease
Beaufighters, which they would fly until 1945 when all
units received the P-61. The 416th was also fortunate
enough to get some Mosquitoes. The 427th NFS went into
combat in the theater in September 1944 but was
transferred to the 10th AF with its P-61s, flying combat
from December 1944 to the end of the war. During the
same period the 426th NFS was transferred from the 10th
to the 14th Air Force, flying combat over China in P-61s.

The 13th Air Force had the 419th NFS operational
with P-70s and P-38s by December 1943. Though the
Lightnings were painted black, they had no radar, which
led to many months of trying to catch Japanese aircraft
(particularly over Guadalcanal) in the blind by ground
searchlight or ground control radar. On the whole this was
not very successful, and it was not until the arrival of the
P-61 that night kills became regular. The 550th NFS went
into combat in January 1945 with P-61s after a mix of
P-70s and P-38s during its early days.

In January and February 1944 the 418th and 421st
Night Fighter Squadrons entered combat with the 5th Air
Force using the standard mix of P-70s and P-38s, and in
their quest to find a truly effective night fighter, the 418th
even used B-25Hs for night attack. Again there was much
frustration until the P-61 arrived late in the year, and a
string of kills began to mount. In October, the 547th NFS
started operations, and by the end of the war a total of
forty-two kills was scored by the three units. The leading
American night fighter ace of the war, 418th pilot Carroll
C. Smith, claimed seven victories and two probables—
three of his kills were scored in the P-38. With his radar
operator Philip Porter, Smith got four of his kills, on two
different missions, during the night of 29/30 December
1944, an unequaled feat among American night fighters.

Extensive night fighter operations were initiated by
the 7th Air Force off Saipan with the 6th NFS in June
1944. Sending detachments to other combat zones, the
unit's P-61s soon began to rack up kills. By September the
548th NFS was in combat with their Black Widows, and
by March 1945 the 549th had joined it at Iwo Jima. The
night fighters followed the front lines to end the war at Ie
Shima. Henry Meigs II, a pilot with the 6th NFS, scored
three night kills in P-61s before being transferred to the
339th FS where he scored another three kills in P-38s. The
successful 6th NFS crew of pilot Dale F. Haberman and
radar operator Raymond Mooney flew their P-61
"Moonhappy" to get four confirmed and one probable.

Both the 422nd and 425th Night Fighter Squadrons
were unique among AAF nocturnal units since they were
never equipped with anything but the Black Widow,
starting with service test YP-61s. Both were in combat
with the 9th Air Force in France by July 1944, hounding
German night intruders with great success. Later both
units used the massive firepower of their Black Widows
for tactical ground attack, particularly against trains. The
9th's first night fighter ace was Paul A. Smith of the 422nd
who shot down five aircraft and one V-1 flying bomb.
The 9th AF produced two other aces (both from the
422nd) who downed five aircraft each—Herman E. Ernst
and Eugene D. Axtell.

Though a night fighter version of the Lightning, the P-38M, was produced from line P-38Ls they arrived in the Pacific too late to see combat.

The U.S. Navy produced several night fighter aces who flew radar-equipped Grumman F6F Hellcats, among them Russell L. Reiserer who scored nine kills, eight with VF(N)-76, William E. Henry who got 9.5 victories with VF(N)-41, Fred L. Dugan of VF(N)-76 with seven kills and another Fighting 76 pilot, John W. Dear, with seven

kills. Unfortunately, the USN ban on additional markings held true with most of the night fighter units so nose art was very rare.

Though hunting other aircraft in the dark with radar and sharp eyes was in its infancy during World War II, pilots and radar operators proved very adaptable indeed, writing the first chapter in what has now become the accepted method of fighter combat.

JEANNIE LOUISE II, a Bristol Beaufighter MK V1F of the 416th Night Fighter Squadron, Grottaglie, Italy, November 1943. Aircraft was painted dark green and medium gray. The Beaufighter was the principal U.S. nightfighter in the MTO until the Black Widow arrived. *Jerry McKee*

1 o'clock jump, a F6F-5N of VMF (N)-541 parked with two other Hellcat's adorned with lovely ladies. Equipped with radar for night fighting and armed with two 20mm cannon and four .50 cal. machine guns, the Hellcat proved to be a formidable opponent. Photo taken on Falalop Island, May 30, 1945. *Grumman via L. Lobisolo*

BLACK WIDOW, NF, a P-70. The P-70s were modified A-20s, with radar for night fighting. *AFM*

BLACK MAGIC, a P-61 piloted by Capt. J. C. Jenkins. The Northrop P-61 replaced the Beaufighter in the Mediterranean Theater in January 1945. *AFM*

MOONHAPPY, a P-61 piloted by Lt. Dale F. Haberman of the 6th Night Fighter Squadron. The aircraft was named for its Radar Operator, Ray Mooney and Pilot, Dale "Hap" Haberman. Lt. Haberman destroyed four Bettys and has a probable on a Kate. *Witte, via Crow*

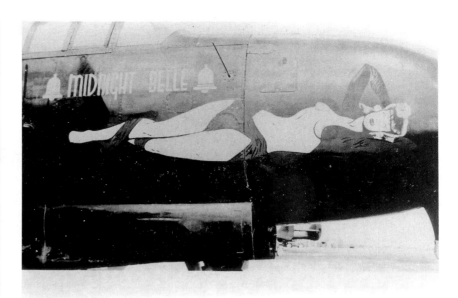

MIDNIGHT BELLE, a P-61 piloted by Capt. Mark E. Martin of the 6th Night Fighter Squadron, 1944. *AFM*

The 'Virgin' Widow, a P-61 of the 6th NFS. The cherries enclosing the name are a characteristic of Eldon T. Gladden's nose art. Other examples of his art are: *MIDNIGHT BELLE*, (bells enclose the name) and *MOONHAPPY* (crescent moons enclose the name). *AFM*

Jukin' Judy, a P-61 piloted by 1st Lt. E. Lee, Radar Operator A. Dorner and Crew Chief E. Jevyak of the 422nd Night Fighter Squadron, 9th Air Force. *AFM*

Lady In The Dark, a P-61B-15 (s/n 42-39713) of the 548th Night Fighter Squadron. This aircraft was attacked after the formal surrender of Japan by two Japanese aircraft—which *Lady In the Dark* summarily dispatched. *AFM*

A line-up of Black Widows, each showing the insignia of the 548th Night Fighter Squadron, a cat carrying a flashlight and a smoking revolver. They are parked on a ramp at Iwo Jima between missions. *AFM*

COOPER'S SNOOPER, a P–61 piloted by Lt. George C. Cooper of the 548th Night Fighter Squadron. Picture taken on Iwo Jima in April 1945. *AFM*

"WABASH CANNON–BALL IV", the first P–61 in Europe. It was shot down by British aircraft that did not recognize it.

Nightie Mission, a P–61 of the 6th Night Fighter Squadron, 7th Fighter Command, Ie Shima, 1945. *Witte, via Crow*

Sleepy Time Gal, a P–61 of the 422nd Night Fighter Squadron. The man in the middle is Mickey Rooney. *AFM*

"*Lovely Lady*", a P–61 of the 422nd Night Fighter Squadron, 9th Air Force. *AFM*

"SHOO-SHOO-BABY", a P–61 of the 422nd Night Fighter Squadron, 9th Air Force, 1944. *SHOO-SHOO-BABY* was the first P–61 delivered to the 422nd in England. *AFM*

WACKY WABBIT, a P–61 after the port landing gear collapsed. Note the rabbit is trying to communicate a message. Another finger was added later to form a V for victory. *Clark, via Crow*

WACKY WABBIT, showing the same rabbit as before, but with the second finger of victory. WACKY WABBIT was a member of the 422nd Night Fighter Squadron, 9th Air force. The 422nd was awarded two DUCs. *AFM*

This port side view of WACKY WABBIT has only the name without the artwork. WACKY WABBIT was written off after this accident and used for spare parts. *Crow*

This wheel cover on WACKY WABBIT is decorated with the figure of a lady inside a star shaped background, confirming that there were few parts of the airplane too small for artwork. *Crow*

MOONLIGHT WRECK-WIZISHUN, a P–61 of the 422nd Night Fighter Squadron. This P–61 was the recipient of the nose from WACKY WABBIT. *Crow*

No Love! NO NOTHING!, a P–61A (s/n 42–5558) piloted by Lt. Col. Oris B. Johnson of the 422nd Night Fighter Squadron. Johnson is credited with a Fw 190, October 24, 1944, and a Ju 188, December 27, 1944. *AFM*

A later version of the nose art *No Love! NO NOTHING!* featuring the faces of five young lovelies. Lt. Col. Johnson stands in the cockpit.

WANDERIN, a P–61 of the 422nd Night Fighter Squadron. *Crow*

SLEEPY TIME GAL, a P–61 of the 422nd Night Fighter Squadron. *AFM*

"DOUBLE TROUBLE", a P–61A (s/n 42–5565) piloted by Lt. Robert G. Bolinder of the 422nd Night Fighter Squadron. Bolinder's radar operator was R. F. Graham and crew chief was E. W. McLain. Bolinder is credited with four aerial victories, one in *DOUBLE TROUBLE*. *Bolinder, via Crow*

A closer view of the nose art *"DOUBLE TROUBLE."*

"Impatient WIDOW", a P-61 of the 422nd Night Fighter Squadron, damaged in combat with an He 177 the evening of August 14, 1944. Its right engine and hydraulic system were shot out. The He 177 got away, but not without being hit. *Clark, via Crow*

"Lady GEN", the top scoring P-61 of the 422nd Fighter Squadron. Pictured in the middle is Brigadier General Elwood "Pete" R. Quesada. On either side of the general are officers of the 422nd—all of whom are wearing the DFC. *Clark, via Crow*

"Lady GEN" after crashing while on a training flight over Kassel, Germany, May 6, 1945. The pilot and crew of the *Lady GEN* are the same as *JUKIN' Judy:* Pilot Capt. E. Lee, Radar Operator A. Dorner, and Crew Chief E. Jevyak. Clark, via Crow

"HUSSLIN HUSSEY", a P-61 of the 422nd Night Fighter Squadron, 9th Air Force. *Clark, via Crow*

The completed artwork on "HUSSLIN HUSSEY".

TACTLESS TEXAN, a P-61 of the 422nd Night Fighter Squadron, 9th Air Force. *Clark, via Crow*

A P-61 piloted by Capt. W. T. Bradley. Artwork showing a dancing six legged lady representative of a black widow spider. Above the artwork is a Japanese flag, denoting the destruction of an enemy aircraft. *AFM*

THE GREAT SPECKLED BIRD, a P-61 of the 422nd Night Fighter Squadron, 9th Air Force. *Cheske, via Crow*

"BORROWED TIME", a P-61 of the 422nd Night Fighter Squadron with the grim reaper under the name. Note the shark mouth on this Black Widow. *Crow*

Another photo of *"BORROWED TIME"*, sans shark mouth nose art. Parked nearby are British Mosquitoes. The P-61s have D-Day stripes on their wings and twin booms. The Mosquitoes have them on their wings and empennage. *Crow*

VEUVE NOIRE, a P-61 on display. Note the figure of the black widow partially obscured by a prop. Also of interest is the crescent moon and broom, denoting night fighter sweeps. *AFM*

TENNESSEE RIDGE RUNNER, a P-61, (s/n 42–5543) of the 422nd Night Fighter Squadron, 9th Air Force, Scorton, England, 1944. *Anderson, via Crow*

"Laura Lil", a P-61 of the 422nd Night Fighter Squadron, 9th Air Force. *Clark, via Crow*

MIDNIGHT MENACE, a P-61 of the 422 Night Fighter Squadron, 9th Air Force. *Clark, via Crow*

Midnight Wrekwisition, a P-61 of the 422nd Night Fighter Squadron, 9th Air Force. Photo taken near Florennes, Belgium, September 1944. *Koehler, via Crow*

FEARLESS FOSDICK, *Writ By Hand*, a P-61. Group and squadron unknown. *AFM*

With a P-61 of the 422nd Night Fighter Squadron sporting the name Mildred on the port engine cowling in the background, this ground crewman reads the news. The headlines of *THE STARS AND STRIPES* says it all. *Crow*

SHARK II, an F–5E of the 12th Photo Recon Squadron, 3rd Photo Recon Group. Pictured are Crew Chief Mike Margarita (center), and other members of the ground crew. *Campbell*

Reconnaissance - alone, unarmed and unafraid

When the airplane first went to war it was considered somewhat fragile and ineffective—except as an observation and photo reconnaissance platform. World War I observation pilots with vertical cameras could bring home more crucial information in less time than any other intelligence gathering operation. Since that time the strategies of war have depended heavily on the data recorded by those who have been willing to fly, for the most part, unarmed aircraft into enemy territory.

At the time of Pearl Harbor, the US had several photo recon squadrons and a single photo group as the AAF was slowly transitioning from older observation groups. The premier American photo recce aircraft of the war was the Lockheed F-4/F-5 series (a camera nosed versions of the Lightning fighter). Usually lighter than their fighter brethren, these photo ships ranged throughout every theater with the ability to fly higher and faster than most enemy fighters—and when necessary, Photo Joes could get right down on the deck to elude anti-aircraft fire and outrun prowling fighters.

The first outfit into combat was Karl Polifka's 8th Photo Squadron at Melbourne, Australia in April 1942. By July they were flying from Port Moresby mapping large portions of eastern New Guinea and eastern New Britain. Polifka and his "Eight Balls," as the squadron came to be known, managed to elude most enemies except one—the far deadlier tropical weather. On the way up to Rabaul the F-4s had to cross the equatorial front with its attendant towering cumulus and low ceilings.

As the war progressed, full strength photo groups were assigned to each theater and were crucial to the success of Allied operations. Unfortunately, the risks to recce pilots have never been headline making news. Unarmed and usually without fighter escort protection, they flew over heavily defended targets while having to hold a steady course over the objective. During the early war years many pilots were lost due to inadequate oxygen equipment when flying above 30,000 feet. When a pilot did not return, there was no heroic story to be sent in for a decoration, quite simply he became another statistic. One of the more successful units was the 8th Air Force's 7th Photo Group which flew Lightnings, Spitfires and finally Mustangs.

Much long-range reconnaissance was accomplished by modified bombers which could carry an almost unlimited amount of film to feed multiple cameras. The B-24, which became the F-7, was ideally suited for flying across Pacific expanses to distant objectives. The number of conversions grew to an impressive list: F-3 (A-20), F-8 (Mosquito), F-9 (B-17), F-10 (B-25) and F-13 (B-29), among others.

The impressive exception to the unarmed recce aircraft was the F-6 Mustang which retained the .50 caliber machine guns of the P-51 when cameras were added. With it came a new designation—tactical reconnaissance—which gave the units the mission freedom to engage the enemy with more than film.

In July 1944, the 9th Air Force's 67th Tactical Recon Group's four squadrons were intermixed with the four of the 10th Photo Group to form a balance of two photo and two tactical squadrons for assignment to the 1st and 3rd Armies on the continent. With the arrival of additional armies more tactical units were attached until any field commander could film and strafe just about anything he desired. A total of three tac recce aces emerged from the 9th AF (all with the 15th TRS): Clyde B. East (twelve kills), John H. Hoefker (8.5) and Leland A. Larson (six).

The 12th Air Force's 3rd and 5th Photo Recon Groups roamed the Mediterranean with the help of the 68th Observation Group (A-20s, P-39s, B-17s) which included the 111th and 154th Tac Recon Squadrons attached with Mustangs. Numerous kills were scored by these units, but they produced no aces.

The 10th Air Force's 8th Photo Group had the 20th Tac Recon Squadron attached with P-40s and F-6s. The recon unit in the theater was the 14th Air Force's 21st Photo Recon Squadron (PRS) with Lightnings. The balance of these units and aircraft proved to be ideal for the ever changing front lines in the CBI.

In mid January 1944, the 28th PRS joined the 7th Air Force, followed by the 41st PRS in April 1945—both units flew F-5s to XXI Bomber Command and 20th Air Force targets for coverage of the very long range missions launched against Japan.

Over the Pacific expanses covered by the 5th Air Force, the 6th Photo Group flew F-5s and F-7s. The 71st Tac Recon Group entered combat in November 1943 with P-39s, re-equipped with P-40s in late 1944 and finally received F-6s in November. The only 5th AF tac recon ace, 110th TRS pilot William A. Shomo, got seven of his eight kills in his F-6D on a single mission, 11 January 1945, which earned him the Medal of Honor.

The variety of missions and aircraft in the photo and tac recon groups produced some of the more unique examples of nose art during the war, particularly on Lightnings. As with its fighter counterpart, the aircraft provided more than enough room for artistic expression.

SNOOPER, an F-5, the famous "souped up" No. 303 with her crew chief, Sgt. P. F. Miller, at A-46 Toussus-Le-Noble, France. *P-38 National Association, via Joe Kuhn*

Super Snooper, an F-5 of the 30th Photo Recon Squadron, with Crew Chief Sgt. Thomas Bowen, at Eschwege, Germany, April 14, 1945. The aircraft markings show nine photo missions, three high-level recon missions, four escort missions and nine dicing missions. *AFM*

SHARK, an F-5 (s/n 42-13095) of the 12th Photo Recon Squadron, 3rd Photo Recon Group, 12th Air Force, with Crew Chiefs Mike Margarita (left) and Ralph Willet, in Siena, Italy, August 1944. *P-38 National Association, via Joe Kuhn*

The starboard side of SHARK showing the name *Vera* on the engine cowl. This side was named for a nurse in the states who corresponded with Crew Chief Ralph Willet. *Willet*

The starboard side of SHARK II also carries the name *VERA* on the engine cowl, however the name on the nose has been changed to *BOOTS*. SHARK II had red spinners with white hubs. This picture was taken in Florence, Italy, May 1945. *Willett*

Missouri Outlaw, an F-5 of the 28th Photo Recon Squadron, 7th Photo Recon Group, 7th Air Force. This ship is a veteran of seventy-one recon missions. Picture taken at the airfield on Iwo Jima, March 1944. *AFM*

LUCKY LU, an F-5B and *Stinky*, an F-5B—both of the 28th Photo Recon Squadron, 7th Photo Recon Group. Photo taken on Saipan, August 29, 1944. *LUCKY LU* is showing a pair of dice marking a low level recon mission. *Lemke, via Crow*

Missouri Outlaw, an F-5B with the 28th Photo Recon Squadron, 7th Photo Recon Group. *Dool, via Crow*

AWAITING AUTUMN, an F-5 of the 28th Photo Recon Squadron, 7th Photo Recon Group. The curled prop on only one side indicates one landing gear collapsed during landing. *Dool, via Crow*

BLACK NICK, an F-4 piloted by Capt. G. N. Dragnick. *AFM*

NAUGHTY NITA, an F-4 piloted by Lt. C. J. Lerable. *AFM*

ISABELLE II, an F-4 piloted by Lt. S. W. Thurber. *AFM*

"mitchell deb", an F–5 (s/n 44–25175) of the 28th Photo Recon Squadron, 7th Photo Recon Group. This aircraft was named by its crew chief, James Schuhl. Note the beckoning hand, inviting glance and smile. *P–38 National Association, via Joe Kuhn*

The Texas Flipper, an F–5 of the 21st Photo Recon Squadron, China. *AFM*

Cactus Jack, an F–5 of the 21st Photo Recon Squadron, China. *AFM*

Jayhawk, an F–5 of the 21st Photo Recon Squadron, China. *AFM*

DOTTIE, an F–5 of the 28th Photo Recon Squadron, 7th Photo Recon Group. Markings show this plane to be a veteran of 140 missions. *P–38 National Association, via Joe Kuhn*

Geronimo II, an F–5 of the 21st Photo Recon Squadron, China. *AFM*

ROWDY RITA, an F-5 of the 25th Photo Recon Squadron, 6th Photo Recon Group, 5th Air Force. The pilot, Capt. D. D. Donham, named his aircraft after his wife, Rita. Capt. Donham's crew chief was T/Sgt. F. R. Janego. *Paul Fournet*

Shamrock II, an F-5 of the 21st Photo Recon Squadron. This picture was taken in China. *AFM*

An F-5, (s/n 44-26441) piloted by Lt. Lyle Bunce of the 25th Photo Recon Squadron, 6th Photo Recon Group, 5th Air Force. The nose art shows an outhouse between two buzz saws, an illustration of Bunce's opinion of the F-5. *Paul Fournet*

A close-up view of the nose art on *Geronimo II*.

MEXICAN SPITFIRE, an F-5 (s/n 44-25826) piloted by Lt. M. G. Basbas of the 25th Photo Recon Squadron, 6th Photo Recon Group. *MEXICAN SPITFIRE'S* crew chief was Sgt. C. R. Spoufe. *Paul Fournet*

VILLANOVA WILDCAT, an F-5 piloted by Capt. Ed Conway of the 25th Photo Recon Squadron, 6th Photo Recon Group. Capt. Conway named his aircraft in honor of his alma mater. *VILLANOVA WILDCAT's* crew chief was Sgt. W. S. Rose. *Paul Fournet*

CACTUS Jack II, an F-5 piloted by Lt. Ed Van Fleet of the 25th Photo Recon Squadron, 6th Photo Recon Group. "Van" is a Nevada rancher and this is his trademark. *Paul Fournet*

THE COMELY COOLIE, an F-5 of the 28th Photo Recon Squadron, 7th Photo Recon Group, 8th Air Force. This aircraft was named for Crew Chief Leslie Coolie. P-38 *National Association, via Joe Kuhn*

SNOOPERMAN, an F-5 of the 34th Photo Recon Squadron, 10th Photo Recon Group, 9th Air Force. Photo recon missions are marked by swastikas on this plane. *Zemanek, via Crow*

Queenie, an F-5 piloted by Lt. William C. Clevenger of the 33rd Photo Recon Squadron, 10th Photo Recon Group. *Clevenger, via Crow*

SWEET DREAM, an F-5 of the 33rd Photo Recon Squadron, 10th Photo Recon Group. Pictured is S/Sgt. Emil Proska standing by the many mission marks earned by this aircraft. *Proska, via Crow*

Lascivious Lady, an F-5 of the 33rd Photo Recon Squadron, 10th Photo Recon Group. Photo taken at Chalgrove, England, in mid 1944. *Proska, via Crow*

STAR DUST, an F-5 in Japan during 1945. *Boehime, via Crow*

An F-6 of the 161st Tactical Recon Squadron, 363rd Tactical Group, 9th Air Force. *Wolf, via Crow*

REX, an F-6 of the 161st Tactical Recon Squadron, 363rd Tactical Group. Standing on the wing is the pilot, Lt. Vesley. *Wolf, via Crow*

Puss Boots, an F-5 of the 33rd Photo Recon Squadron, 10th Photo Recon Group, 9th Air Force. Pictured here is Capt. William C. Clevenger, who was the pilot of the F-5, *Queenie*. *Proska, via Crow*.

Puss in Boots 2, an F-5 of the 33rd Photo Recon Squadron, 363rd Tactical Recon Group, 9th Air Force. *Proska, via Crow*

The OUTLAW, an F-5 of the 31st Photo Recon Squadron, 10th Photo Recon Group. *Moher, via Crow*

Naughty Dotty, an F-5 stationed in the Pacific. *Crow*

GREEN EYES, an F-5, group and squadron unknown. *P-38 National Association, via Kuhn*

Eyes of TEXAS, an F–5. Note the manned photo pod under the port wing. *AFM*

LILA MAY, an F–5 of the 31st Photo Recon Squadron, 9th Air Force. *Elliott, via Crow*

"Haughty–Helen", an F–5 of the 34th Photo Recon Squadron, 69th Tactical Recon Group, 9th Air Force, stationed in Germany, on April 24, 1945. Note the name *IRENE* on the engine cowl. Helen was the pilot's girlfriend and Irene was the crew chief's wife. *Sodergren, via Crow*

Snooks, a P–39 seen here on March 5, 1944 with Sgt. Ralph Winkle, crew chief. This P–39 was 1st Lt. William Shomo's ship, assigned to the 71st Recon Squadron of the 82nd Recon Group. Lt. Shomo is credited with eight aerial victories. *via E. McDowell*

The FLYING UNDERTAKER, an F–6 (44–2505) piloted by Captain William A. Shomo. He earned his first aerial victory (a Val) on January 10, 1945. The following day he destroyed a Betty and six Tonys, earning the Congressional Medal of Honor. *B. Hess*

Nose art from an F–5 piloted by 1st Lt. F. B. Eckenrode of the 33rd Photo Recon Squadron, 10th Photo Recon Group, 9th Air Force. Lt. Eckenrode was killed in action December 25, 1944, over Germany. *Proska, via Crow*

Shark's teeth on the starboard engine cowl of an F-5 piloted by Lt. William C. Clevenger of the 33rd Photo Recon Squadron, 9th Air Force. *Clevenger, via Crow*

Tampa JOE, an F-6 of the 12th Recon Squadron piloted by Leo Elliott. Elliott shot down one Ju 87 Stuka and has half credit for a kill on a Ju 88. *Elliott, via T. Ivey*

The NINA MAE, an F-5 of the 21st Photo Recon Squadron, China. *AFM*

PRIDE OF THE BLUEGRASS, an F-6 (code AM-D) of the 12th Recon Squadron. Pictured (left to right) are Lt. Bill Davenport, 1.5 victories; Lt. John Ellis, Jr., two victories; Lt. Lefebure, one aircraft damaged.

MAZIE, ME AND MONK, an F-6 of the 12th Recon Squadron (code ZM-O) piloted by Capt. E. B. "Blackie" Travis, shown with his crew chief S/Sgt. Monk Davidson. This aircraft located lost Allied troops while flying in impossible weather during the Battle of the Bulge. *J. Davidson, via T. Ivey*

BEAVER, an F-5 of the 21st Photo Recon Squadron, China. *AFM*

Moby DICK, an F-5 of the 21st Photo Recon Squadron, China. *AFM*

Bob Hope and Jerry Colona christening the F-6C named in their honor. *Moher, via Crow*

SHOVELNOSE AND HANDLEBAR, an F-6C (code ZM-E, s/n 42-103613) piloted by Edward J. Kenny III of the 162nd Tactical Reconnaissance Squadron, 10th Photo Recon Group, 9th Air Force. The crew chief was J. L. Roberts. *Moher, via Crow*

Oh Johnie, an F-6C (s/n 43-25081) piloted by Lt. Childers. *Oh Johnie's* crew chief was Cpl. duFosse. *Crow*

The fighter nose art of the Korean War was similar in many ways to
World War II nose art.

Korea

With the end of World War II the US went into a period of rapid change . . . propellers gave way to jets and the "Hot Rock Fighter Pilot" became the "Jet Jockey." By 1950, without much fanfare, Americans were again at war, only this time in the first of many nebulous undeclared conflicts which had no clear military mandate for victory. The US would be involved in the Korean Police Action for three years under the worst of conditions.

The fighter pilots who went to fly combat with the Far East Air Force (FEAF) found some of the old types from the war as well as the newest machines which could fly higher, faster and farther. As with their airplanes, some of these pilots were not new guys on the block. Many had already run up victory credits—Jabara, Davis, Baker, Johnson, Garrison, Hagerstrom, Gabreski, Bolt, Whisner, Creighton, Thyng, Mahurin, Eagleston, to name a few.

The warpaint didn't change much, though the advance of a few years seemed to splash more sexually explicit art across many machines, causing FEAF censorship to become an active process. The cartoon characters from Warner Brothers and Disney Studios were back, along with the youthful blood and guts bravado.

In opposing the Communist forces of North Korea, China and the Soviet Union, Americans were joined by South Koreans, South Africans, Australians, Britons and several other free nationalities, some in units of their own: No. 2 Squadron, South African Air Force, flew F–51s and F–86s; No. 77 Squadron, Royal Australian Air Force, flew F–51s and Meteors; No. 91 (Comp) Wing, Royal Navy, flew Sea Furys and Fireflys. The USAF, USN, USMC and US Army were all tasked to fly in support of UN forces, primarily in ground attack and resupply.

In the course of three years the destruction visited by USAF crews was extensive: 963 locomotives, over 10,000 railroad cars, 1,327 tanks, 1,153 bridges, 28,621 rail cuts and 8,863 gun positions. In the air-to-air arena the kill totals ran to more than 900 destroyed, 169 probables, 975 damaged while less than 150 aircraft were claimed on the ground.

America's only dedicated air-to-air fighter was the F–86 Sabre, which accounted for 810 of the aerial claims with the USAF 4th and 51st Fighter Interceptor Wings and the 8th and 18th Fighter Bomber Wings. Of the 40 aces produced by the war, the leaders were Joseph McConnell (16 kills, 51st Wing), James Jabara (15 kills, 4th Wing) and Pete Fernandez (14.5 kills, 4th Wing). Hunting, for the most part, had to be done at long range near the Yalu River where MiG–15 pilots sought sanctuary from the roving bands of Sabres.

Though US Navy pilots, flying from carriers in the South China Sea, did not get much opportunity to mix it up with enemy aircraft, they scored sixteen aerial and thirty-six ground victories while dropping 120,000 tons of bombs. The Marines, flying extensive ground support, racked up thirty-five aerial victories.

Though the night fighter war was not extensive, F–94Bs of the 319th Fighter Interceptor Squadron claimed four victories, Marines flying F7Fs, F4Us and F3Ds made eleven kills and Navy Lt. Guy Bordelon became a night ace with five kills in an F4U–5N. Though some of the adversaries were MiGs, for the most part the enemy aircraft were propeller driven "Bedcheck Charlies" which made nuisance light bombing raids designed to keep people awake.

The end of the Korean War brought an abrupt end to nose art as it had been known. Almost overnight the benign tolerance for crews in warzones painting almost anything on their aircraft turned into a dedicated peacetime campaign to make sure it never reappeared. Though some did surface here and there and the Vietnam War led to similar lapses in censorship, on the whole the warpaint of World War II and Korea will never be back. Today current USAF units are reapplying some of the genre's classic examples to their aircraft in honor of heroes now gone. Unfortunately those which portray women have resulted in angry cries from feminists without a knowledge of history. They say the art is another example of men degrading women to objects and should be removed, but they miss the point. No doubt about it. As an era has disappeared, so has the warpaint that stood for a generation of warriors who were willing to sacrifice their lives in the cause of freedom. God bless 'em all.

BAD CHECK ALWAYS COMES BACK, an F–51 (s/n 47–4723) piloted by Jim Gasser. *Jim Gasser, via Jeff Ethell*

Striking power is vividly portrayed by this long line of heavily armed US Air Force F–51 Mustangs of the Fifth Air Force's veteran 18th Fighter-Bomber Wing in Korea. *Jeff Ethell*

THE HUFF, an F–86F, (code FU–897) piloted by Lt. Jim Thompson of the 39th Fighter Interceptor Squadron. Lt. Thompson is credited with destroying two MiG–15s.

My Boots, a B–26 Invader assigned to the 3rd Bombardment Group. Pictured is Sgt. William K. "Bill" O'Neil at K–14 in South Korea. *O'Neil*

Paper Tiger/HEAVENS ABOVE, an F–86F piloted by Capt. Harold Fischer of the 39th FIS. Fischer destroyed ten MiG–15s before being shot down and held as a POW. He was not released until twenty-two months after the armistice.

Margie, an F-86F piloted by Capt. Lonnie R. Moore of the 335th Fighter Interceptor Squadron, 4th Fighter Interceptor Wing. Margie was the name of Capt. Moore's wife. The other side of the aircraft carried the name of his son Billy. Capt. Moore destroyed ten MiG-15s.

"Funfrus", an F-86 piloted by Lt. Col. William Cosby, CO of the 334th Fighter Interceptor Squadron, 4th Fighter Wing. The insignia on the side is a carryover from the famous 4th Fighter Group "Debden Eagles" of WWII. Lt. Col. Cosby is credited with three MiG-15s.

Liza Gal/El Diablo, an F-86 piloted by Maj. Chuck Owens of the 336th Fighter Interceptor Squadron, 4th Fighter Interceptor Wing. Maj. Owens is credited with two MiG-15s. The aircraft shows eight stars for MiGs, one tank and fifteen trucks.

A later photo of *El Diablo* showing more complete art and another MiG kill.

JOLLEY ROGER, an F-86 piloted by Capt. Clifford D. Jolley of the 335th Fighter Interceptor Squadron, 4th Fighter Interceptor Wing. Capt. Jolley is credited with seven MiG kills.

Flying Jenny, an F-86E (s/n 51-0684) of the 4th Fighter Interceptor Wing.

Dude, an F–86F (s/n 51–12976) piloted by Lt. Craig Fink of the 335th Fighter Interceptor Squadron, 4th Fighter Interceptor Wing.

SUNNY, an F–86 of the 51st Fighter Interceptor Wing being prepped for a mission on a cold Korean winter day.

MIG MAD MARINE/LYN, ANNE, DAVE, an F–86F of the 25th Fighter Interceptor Squadron piloted by Maj. John Glenn, USMC. Maj. Glenn shot down three MiGs while temporarily assigned to the 25th Squadron. Lyne, Anne, and Dave are his wife's name and children's names.

CAROLINA MOON, a B–26 Invader assigned to the 3rd Bombardment Group and used for ground attack.

OL' NADSOB an F–51D (s/n 45–11742) of the 67th Fighter Bomber Squadron, 18th Fighter Bomber Group.

THE IRON CHIT BIRD and *BAD PENNY,* both F–51s, are parked but ready for duty.

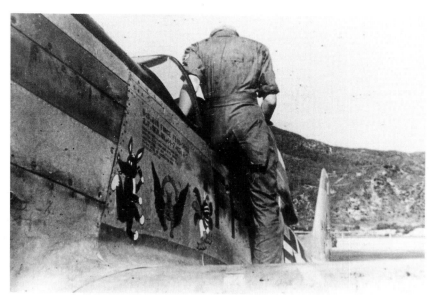

The pilot of this F–51 of the 67th Fighter Bomber Squadron is preparing for the next mission.

Tulie, Scotty & ?, an RF–51K (code RF–913) piloted by Lt. B. W. Scott of the 45th Tactical Recon Squadron. The Squadron was originally formed as the 423rd Fighter Squadron on August 17, 1943. *Jeff Ethell*

"BETTY JANE", an RF–51, (code FF–517) of the 45th Tactical Recon Squadron stationed at Kimpo. Note the polka dotted spinner, a trademark of the 45th. *Jeff Ethell*

Taking off are members of the 12th Fighter Bomber Squadron, 18th Fighter Bomber Group, stationed at Chinhae, Korea. The planes of the squadron carried the familiar shark mouth design. *Mark Bacon*

O'L ANCHOR ASS, an F–51 flown by Maj. William O'Donnell, the CO of the 36th Fighter Bomber Squadron. O'Donnell had served in the 335th Fighter Squadron, 4th Fighter Group, in WW II during which time he shot down an Me 109 and shared a kill on an Fw 190. *Jeff Ethell*

MAC'S REVENGE, the port side of *O'L ANCHOR ASS*, piloted by Maj. William O'Donnell. *Jeff Ethell*

ZERO ZERO, an F-82F Twin Mustang (code FQ-381) of the 4th F(AW)Squadron. The F-82 scored three of the first seven aerial victories of the Korean Conflict on June 27, 1950. *Jeff Ethell*

Nina, an F-86, (code FU-832) piloted by Col. John Mitchell of the 39th Fighter Interceptor Squadron. Col. Mitchell is credited with four MiG-15s. *Jeff Ethell*

An F9F Panther of VF-783, (the "Minutemen"). This isn't the best way to land, but at least the pilot made it. *Bill Hawthorne*

An F9F Panther of VF-783 Minutemen onboard the *Oriskany* in 1952. The aircraft also had trouble landing. *Bill Hawthorne*

"*BUGS BUCKET O' BOLTS*", a P-80 Shooting Star assigned to a training squadron at March Field, California before the Korean War. *Billy Watson*

STINKER III, a P-80, also assigned for training pilots at March Field, California, before the war. *Billy Watson*

MINIMUM GOOSE, a P-80, March Field. *Billy Watson*

ARCHANGEL, a P-80, March Field. *Billy Watson*

Shooting Star, a P-80 during flight tests at Wright Field, Dayton, Ohio. The pilot is famed World War II ace, Don Gentile (19.83 aerial victories). Like Richard Bong (forty aerial victories), Gentile was killed when the P-80 he was test flying crashed.

Wee Stud, an F-80 reconnaissance version of the Shooting Star. This aircraft carries the NATO insignia. The pilot was Col. Robert Baseler. *Warren Bodie*

A Grumman F9F-4 Panther flown by the USMC. *Warren Bodie*

A Vought F4U–4 Corsair with wings folded, giving an excellent view of the rocket rails. *Warren Bodie*

Dolly, an AD–1 assigned to USS *Oriskany*, Carrier Air Group–102, Attack Squadron 923, the "Rough Raiders". The Rough Raiders saw action in Korea. *Bill Hawthorne*

A VF–874 Corsair. Note the squadron insignia. *Bill Hawthorne*

Miss Hayward, an AD–1 assigned to USS *Oriskany*, Carrier Air Group–102, Attack Squadron 923. *Bill Hawthorne*

This is a close-up of VF–874's squadron insignia. *Bill Hawthorne*

Angel Face & The Babes/THE KING, an F-86E (code FU-822, s/n 51-2822) piloted by Col. Royal "King" Baker of the 336 Fighter Interceptor Squadron. Baker is credited with thirteen aerial victories over Korea and 3.5 during WWII. *E. McDowell*

COCHISE/KIPED, an F-86E piloted by Lt. G. J. Wood Jr. of the 336th Fighter Interceptor Squadron. Note the single star, and multiple truck and train kill markings. *E. McDowell*

HONEST JOHN/Stud, an F-86 (code FU-747, s/n 51-2747) piloted by Col. Walker Mahurin of the 336th Fighter Interceptor Squadron. Mahurin is credited with 3.5 MiGs and 20.75 victories in WWII. *E. McDowell*

The Friendly Undertaker, an F-86 piloted by Capt. William J. Ryan of the 334th Fighter Interceptor Squadron. Note the "boxing eagle" emblem—which is a carryover from the 334th in WWII. Capt. Ryan is credited with two aerial victories. *E. McDowell*

Barb, an F-86 piloted by Capt. Ralph S. Parr, Jr. He scored ten aerial victories (nine MiG-15s and one IL-2) during the months of June and July of 1953 and the final aerial victory of the War (an IL-2 on July 27, 1953).

GOPHER PATROL, an F-86 assigned to the 335th Fighter Interceptor Squadron. *E. McDowell*

Index

208